THE SHOOTING SCRIPT ™

THE BIRDCAGE

THE BIRDCAGE

SCREENPLAY BY
ELAINE MAY

FOREWORD WITH
MIKE NICHOLS

A Newmarket Shooting Script ™ Series Book
NEWMARKET PRESS • NEW YORK

Library of Congress Cataloging–in–Publication Data
May, Elaine,
The birdcage: the shooting script / Elaine May.
p. cm.
ISBN 1-55704-277-2
I. Birdcage (Motion picture)   II. Title.
PN1997.B52   1996
791.43' 72—dc20

96-28600
CIP

Quantity Purchases
Companies, professional groups, clubs, and other organizations may qualify for special terms when ordering quantities of this title. For information, write to Special Sales, Newmarket Press, 18 East 48th Street, New York, NY 10017, or call (212) 832-3575.

Book design by Tania Garcia.
Manufactured in the United States of America.

OTHER NEWMARKET FILM BOOKS INCLUDE

The Shawshank Redemption: The Shooting Script
The People vs. Larry Flynt: The Shooting Script
A Midwinter's Tale: The Shooting Script
The Age of Innocence: The Shooting Script
The Sense and Sensibility Screenplay & Diaries
Dead Man Walking: The Shooting Script
Neil Simon's Lost in Yonkers: The Illustrated
 Screenplay of the Film
Bram Stoker's Dracula: The Film and the Legend

Mary Shelley's Frankenstein: The Classic Tale of
 Terror Reborn on Film
Wyatt Earp: The Film and the Filmmakers
Wyatt Earp's West: Images and Words
Dances with Wolves: The Illustrated
 Story of the Epic Film
The Inner Circle: An Inside View of Soviet
 Life under Stalin

CONTENTS

Foreword: Talking with Mike Nichols   vii

Screenplay of *The Birdcage*   1

Stills & Voices   109

About the Cast and Filmmakers   131

Credits   138

PUBLISHER'S NOTE

Mike Nichols has been delighting audiences since he teamed with Elaine May in 1957 to form the now-legendary Nichols and May comedy team. In 1963, he won the first of seven Tony Awards as the Broadway director of *Barefoot in the Park* and has since directed for the stage such critical and popular successes as *The Odd Couple, Plaza Suite, Prisoner of Second Avenue, The Knack, Luv, The Real Thing,* and *Hurlyburly.* His long list of Hollywood credits includes *Who's Afraid of Virginia Woolf?, The Graduate, Carnal Knowledge, Silkwood, Working Girl, Postcards from the Edge,* and *Wolf.*

Never losing sight of his desire to work with Elaine May on a film, Mike Nichols called her when the rights became available to the outrageous French comedy *La Cage aux Folles,* a film they had been wanting to do for fifteen years. He said, "Do you think it's too late to do it?" She said, "Not at all. This is a good time for it." *The Birdcage* became their first-ever collaboration on a feature film. May's screenplay, based on the stage play by Jean Poiret and the script written by Francis Veber, Edouard Molinaro, Marcello Danon, and Jean Poiret, transforms the 70s story, set on the French Riviera, into a 90s contemporary American comedy about family values, set in South Beach, Florida, and Washington, D.C. Nichols assembled a superlative ensemble cast, headed by the brilliant Robin Williams and Nathan Lane as the gay couple with the twenty-year-old son about to be married, and Gene Hackman and Dianne Wiest as the ultra-conservative future in-laws.

United Artists opened the film on March 8, 1996. A stunning critical and box office success, it earned over $187 million worldwide and became the seventh highest grossing film of 1996 in the U.S.

For this book, Elaine May chose her final version of the shooting script for reproduction. It is not a transcription of what's on the screen, but rather the screenplay from which the director and cast worked. "We had a rule on the picture," Nichols says. "The actors would do the written script until I was satisfied and then we would do one take in which they could improvise. Given this cast, there were obviously some improvs that were insanely funny, but didn't fit the story. But there are moments all through the picture that are improvised and were perfect."

The commentaries by Mike Nichols, Robin Williams, Nathan Lane, and others involved in the film that appear in this book were drawn from production notes and interviews conducted before the opening of the film. Jed Dannenbaum conducted some of these interviews and prepared the editorial excerpts for this book. Nichols's comments about directing as well as his love for comedy, his reasons for insisting on a rehearsal period for his movies, and his delight in working once again with Elaine May are particularly worth noting. Over fifty photographs and complete cast and crew credits round out this volume on a film that Gene Shalit introduced in this way: "Three of my favorite words are Nichols and May—and today's joyous news is that now I can say them together again—because they are together again."

FOREWORD

TALKING WITH MIKE NICHOLS

ON COMEDY:

Looking back I realize how important laughs have always been to me. I started out as a comedian, and after that I directed comedies on Broadway. Once I was talking to Bette Midler, when she was just starting out, about some movie, which we didn't end up doing together, and she asked, "Do you do comedy blocking?" And I said, "I don't know. I hope so, whatever it is." But I guess I do do comedy blocking, she was right, and I think I have a pretty easy time thinking of funny things to do. I don't know why.

Even in serious productions I end up finding humor. I did a play called *Death and the Maiden,* a very serious play, and in the beginning of it we were criticized for having too many big laughs. I actually had to go around killing laughs so everybody would understand that we were very serious and so forth. In my view laughs can be in any play or movie. You can have big laughs in *King Lear* because life is both.

I learned very early that the audience asks you this unspoken question: "Why are you telling me this?" You have to have an answer. And "because

it's funny" is a very good answer. That's one of the reasons *The Birdcage* gave us such pleasure. With "it's funny," you can throw in more and then it's funnier and you throw in a little more and it's funnier yet, that sort of chain reaction funny, where the laughter would go straight through a scene and then through the next scene.

ON REHEARSAL:

I always rehearse a movie a couple of weeks, for a number of reasons. One is that you've got to understand and set the shape and the architecture of the story because you'll never be doing it in order again. So you have to find out where the climaxes are and what the journey is, from the beginning to the end, when you can do everything in order, which you can't do while you're shooting.

Then in this case, we had to find the lives of these people in the past and the ways in which they love each other and don't. And we had to sort of create the detail, create the behavior. Turning psychology into behavior is one of the director's jobs, and it's easier for me to encourage it and do it over a rehearsal period than just showing up to shoot.

I also have an acting theory, which is "The Retake Theory." If you work in movies, what happens is you do a very difficult scene and it takes you three days and then somebody calls the next day and says, "Bad news, the lab screwed

ix

it up." And you say, "Oh no, well, we'll do it again at the end of the schedule when we're finished with the other things." And then two and a half months later, you do the scene in fifteen minutes, because it sort of just sat with the actors, unthought about but ripening, and then, after a couple months, they find very easy what was difficult to begin with.

Nobody ever talks, in our kind of work, about downtime. And I think downtime, time not thinking about it and not working on it, is at least as important as all the time that you've spent working on it and thinking about it. Something happens in our brains and our spirits when we're away from things; they grow on their own, they become part of us in the way that real memories and real experiences become part of us.

And I think rehearsal to some extent has that effect: You do things, you don't finish them, you don't have all your emotional crises and finished climaxes, but you rehearse, and then you leave it alone. And it's so long until you get to those scenes again that they have a chance to sort of inhabit the actor and get comfortable there and grow on their own.

Agador, for example, was a black character before we started to shoot. He

was a servant, and his name wasn't Agador. And we tried to cast it and tried to cast it and it wasn't very funny.

At that point I had Hank Azaria in. I had seen him in *Quiz Show*, and I thought he was remarkable. And I said to him, "I've got two parts here, take your choice. There's this news guy, and there's Nathan's dresser." The dresser was in just one scene at the beginning, helping Nathan put on his stockings and so forth. And Hank said, "Oh, I want the dresser." Then we had a reading of the whole thing, and he was hilarious as the dresser. I said to Elaine after the reading, "Let's change the character of the servant. Remember when the doorman was called Agador? We loved that name, why don't we call him Agador and let Azaria play the whole person? There is no dresser, there is no doorman, there's only Agador."

That's how he came to be and how we made him a part of the family. What part of the family is he? It turned out that by the time we shot one scene, he had evolved to being able to tacitly say to Val, the son, "Don't drink out of the bottle, here's a glass." That's what you do in rehearsal, and everything leads to some small piece of behavior.

ON IMPROVISATION:

We had a rule on this picture, which is that the actors would do the written script until I was satisfied, and then they would get a chance to improvise it. And sometimes, of course, they were insanely funny, but I couldn't use it because it just wasn't absolutely the story. Improvisation by definition has to veer from the scene, and Elaine had spent a long time really thinking these scenes out. But all through the picture there are things that are improvised. In the scene coming up the stairs when Robin says he's hurt his ankle, 67 percent of that is improvised. And I could use little things, such as Robin saying, "Oh, you're going to the cemetery with your toothbrush. How Egyptian." "How Egyptian" was Robin's. It made an enormous difference there. And the idea that if it was great enough it would make it into the picture, that was one more challenge that everybody enjoyed.

Improvisation frees you up and injects a certain energy, usually a wild kind of energy. And then even the scripted lines are gassed up, because now it is no holds barred, the rules are off. That's why Mike let us do it. Sometimes you'll find great things, and sometimes it misses, but it puts something new into the mix, a certain fire.

—Robin Williams

ON ELAINE MAY:

The very first time I met Elaine, I was in a play directed by my friend Paul Sills, *Miss Julie*. It was awful. And a very strange thing happened, which is that Sydney J. Harris, the big Chicago critic, came to the University of Chicago where we were doing it and gave it this great review, which had the horrible result that we had to play it for months and months. And when Harris's review first came out, I was walking down the street and I ran into Paul, who was with this interesting looking girl, Elaine, whom I had never met. And I said, "Paul, have you seen this?" and I showed him the review, and Elaine looked over his shoulder and said "Hah!" She knew how lousy *Miss Julie* was, she had seen it. In fact, I remembered her seeing it because she sat in the front row and looked so skeptical and amused that I could barely get through it.

And then the next time I saw her was at the IC station, which is the railroad that you take to go back to the South Side of Chicago where the university is. She was sitting on a bench and I said, "May I sit down?" and she said, in an accent, "If you wish," and we did this whole long spy improvisation. And then we were friends. We did it later on one of the records. But we improvised it in the actual railroad station the first time, before we knew each other.

When we split up there was the usual partner thing. It was not an entirely friendly split-up. And so we spent some years not even being friends, and then we became friends again, and then we became very good friends. Over the years we did things like inaugurations and benefits as performers. And I never made a movie without spending a couple of days listening to her, or having her talk to me and the writer. The best scene in *Heartburn* came from Elaine asking Nora Ephron questions about her father. In the scene with her father in which he says to her "you want fidelity, marry a swan," that all came from Elaine's questioning of Nora about her real father. On *Wolf,* Elaine saved my ass, it's as simple as that. She came and did a fantastic rewrite job. But she very rarely takes credit on movies, and I'm sort of proud she took a credit on *The Birdcage,* because it's so rare.

Of course, who were better improvisationalists than Nichols and May? Mike comes from that school, yet he's a highly disciplined director. He directed me in my happiest experience on Broadway, with Jeremy Irons and Glenn Close in Tom Stoppard's *The Real Thing,* **so I know his language and how he thinks. He has an elegant sensibility and respects when moments are real, when comedy is unforced, when things just happen without moving them into position comedically. He likes to just see it unfold.**

When Mike directs, it's so succinct, and that's true of Elaine, too. In rehearsals, when the actors were going in a certain direction, she would very diplomatically say, "That choice will cost us down the road, even though it's very funny. It's an expensive choice, because you sell out a little on the character here." She and Mike are both so articulate and concise that as an actor you don't over-analyze, you don't intellectualize. It's not an intellectual process.

—Christine Baranski

She's been the most trusted friend, she's been a part of whatever I did and I, to some extent, of what she did. For fifteen years Elaine and I wanted to do *La Cage aux Folles,* because it's such a great plot. And when the rights became available, I called her up and said, "Do you think it's too late to do it?" and she said, "Not at all. This is a good time for it."

It's been a great joy being reunited with Elaine and rediscovering the whole mood of our partnership, a partnership in which if I don't think of something she thinks of it, and vice versa. And we're somehow better working with each other than with other people. I can't completely explain why it took us so long to really work together again. It seems to me life is a series of realizations of something very, very obvious that took you thirty or forty years to get to. I don't know why it takes so long, but it seems to.

ON MAKING MOVIES:

The thing that I love about movies, the reason I don't think I'll ever be tired of them, is that it's this great combination of preparing like crazy, preparing for a year, preparing everything, and then showing up and finding out what's going to happen because you can't control it. You have to hope for a

Elaine's triumph with regard to the script was to ask the question, "How would it be if this story happened right here, right now, in today's society?" She understood that you have to include every possible kind of prejudice in the telling of this story because in the final reconciliation you represent everyone—not just gays and heterosexuals but Jews and gentiles, Democrats and Republicans...one hopes the whole country.

—Mike Nichols

small miracle every day, and that's life. What will today's great surprise be? Or small surprise? And that's what makes it very exciting.

ON THE STORY:

I think it's always been true for audiences, and I include myself, that we love to be taken to another country, a place we've never been, only to discover that it's like home. And I think that's one of the things that's nice about *The Birdcage,* that you go somewhere you haven't been, to men who dress as women, and discover a big surprise: They're not different from us. You make that discovery over and over, both in life and in movies, and it's one of the most pleasurable ones, to make new friends and in effect say, "Oh I see, they're like us." And of course, one of our favorite kinds of laughter is the laughter that says, "Yes! I never thought of that, I agree." That's a great laugh.

I think that the movie, in the end, is about reconciliation. It's the pleasure of seeing two families that are as opposite as families can possibly be and realizing, in the end, that families are families. They turn out to be two happy families—with all the kvetching and complaining and difficulties, they're still happy families.

"THE BIRDCAGE"

by Elaine May

based on the stage play
"La Cage aux Folles," by Jean Poiret,
and the script written by Francis Veber,
Edouard Molinaro, Marcello Danon, and Jean Poiret

6/23/95

FADE IN:

1   HELICOPTER SHOT - THE SEA - DUSK   1

glittering with the reflected light of sunset. Just ahead
is the outline of a city and as we move in, we begin to see
pale sand dotted with tanned bodies, a pastel street filled
with art deco buildings and upscale tourists, and a heavily
trafficked road with a flashing yellow sign that says: <u>NO
CRUISING WHEN THE LIGHT IS FLASHING</u>.

                       VOICES SINGING: OS
          "We are family,
          I got all my sisters and me,
          We are family,
          Get up everybody and sing..."

2   The CAMERA continues on, tracking the buildings now.   2

As it passes each one, a neon sign comes up revealing the
name of the club or restaurant inside. We hear the sounds
of music and voices mixing and blending with the opening
song...until we reach a sign that says: <u>Armand Goldman's
THE BIRDCAGE! - starring THE GOLDMAN GIRLS and STARINA!</u>.

                       VOICES SINGING: OS
              (they are louder now)
          "Everyone can see we're together
          as we walk by,
          And we fly like birds of a feather
          I tell you no lie..."

3   A LITTLE KNOT OF CUSTOMERS STANDS OUTSIDE THE BIRDCAGE   3
mostly couples of various ages, and the CAMERA follows
them as they make their way through the door...

4   INT. THE BIRDCAGE - NIGHT   4

a small, dark room crammed with tables.

ONSTAGE

SIX GIRLS--performing the Opening Number.

                       VOICES ONSTAGE:
          "We are family
          I got all my sisters with me..."

At the door ARMAND GOLDMAN greets a few incoming customers,
then strolls through the club inspecting his domain.

                                 (CONTINUED)

4   CONTINUED: 4

He opens the door to a small kitchen where a kneeling chef
is transferring a chicken breast from the floor back to a
plate. He closes the door, quickly, and moves on. A WAITER
comes up to him.

                    WAITER
          The Kennedys are here again for
          supper--it's the third time this
          week. Shall I give them a free
          round of drinks?

                    ARMAND
          Ted?

                    WAITER
          No, just the younger Kennedys.

                    ARMAND
          I wish we could get Ted.
               (after a beat)
          Give them a free round of coffee.

He starts forward again. When he reaches the area of the
stage, he pulls aside a black velour and steps through.

5   BACKSTAGE   5

Narrow, cramped. Little more than a corridor lined with
cubicles and doors.

A Stage Manager (CYRIL) stands poised, holding a wig and a
costume, his eyes on the stage. Armand walks up to him.

                    ARMAND
          Where's Starina?

                    CYRIL
          Agador just called. She'll be down
          in five. Whoops...

Cyril springs into action as the opening number ends and
one of the girls runs offstage, tearing off her costume
for a quick change. Under the sequined bra is a flat chest.
Under the flowing wig is a crew cut.

Under the little silk skirt is a jock strap made of ace
bandages and tape.

Armand peeks out at the audience.

                    ARMAND
          You know, we should try for three
          shows on Saturday. Look at that
          crowd.

                                              (CONTINUED)

5   CONTINUED: 5

A door in the opposite wall suddenly flies open, missing
the changing performer and Cyril by inches. A dark,
barefoot man in leopard skin shorts (AGADOR) stands on
the bottom step, panting.

                    AGADOR
          Starina won't go on. She's still
          in her robe.

                    ARMAND
          Oh, _damn_.

                    AGADOR
          I don't know _what_ happened this
          time.

                    ARMAND
          Go back upstairs and try to get her
          dressed. I'll be right behind you.
          Oh, _merde_!

Agador turns and hurries through the door up the stairs.
Armand turns to Cyril.

                    ARMAND
          Cyril! Tell Carmen to get ready to
          do Starina's number, just in case.
          You understand?

                    CYRIL
          Don't be stern. I'll fall apart.
          Oh, my God!

6   INT. BEDROOM/DRESSING ROOM - STARINA   6

clutching a flimsy robe about him as he faces Agador.

                    AGADOR
               (holding out high heels
                and stockings)
          Just put these on. Please.

                    ALBERT
          No, Agador. Victoria Page will not
          dance the dance of the red shoes
          tonight. Or any other night.

                    AGADOR
          Just the stockings.

                    ALBERT
          Victoria Page is dead.

                    AGADOR
          Just _this_ stocking...

                                              (CONTINUED)

6 CONTINUED: 6

> ALBERT
> Do you know how she died?
> (he laughs softly)
> Alone. Weeping for her lover.
> "For each man kills the thing he
> loves..." Have you eaten? You
> look haggard.

> AGADOR
> Please...

> ALBERT
> (handing him a fistful of
> packets)
> Here. These are supplements. I
> bought them for Armand but...
> (his eyes fill)
> ...that's all over now.

7 INT. STAIRS LEADING TO THE APARTMENT - ARMAND   7

hurries up the last few stairs and opens the door, revealing
a living room. He walks in and calls:

> ARMAND
> Albert!

8 STARINA'S ROOM   8

Starina screams...then runs to the door and, before Agador
can stop him, locks it and leans against it. Armand begins
knocking.

> ARMAND'S VOICE
> Come on, Albert, open the door.

> ALBERT
> Get out!

> ARMAND'S VOICE
> Albert! Open it!

Armand's knocking grows louder.

> AGADOR
> Let's open the door for him, shall
> we? Let's be nice.

> ALBERT
> No. I don't want him to see me.
> I'm hideous.

The door suddenly bursts open and Armand stands there,
holding his shoulder. Starina screams wildly, then runs to
the window and covers himself with a curtain.

(CONTINUED)

8 CONTINUED: 8

                              ARMAND
                    Do you want to ruin me?

                              ALBERT
                    Don't look at me. I'm hideous!
                    Hideous! Fat and hideous. Oh,
                    Agador. I'm in such pain...

                              AGADOR
                    I know. It will pass.

                              ALBERT
                    It will never pass. I hate my
                    life! Don't forget to take those
                    supplements.

                              ARMAND
                    Are you crazy! Do you realize that
                    there's a packed house out there--

                              ALBERT
                    That's all I am to you, isn't it?
                    A meal ticket.

                              ARMAND
                         (closing his eyes)
                    I can't stand this!

                              ALBERT
                    Never mind about my feelings.
                    Never mind about my suffering.
                    It's just about "your show." Not
                    even "our" show. "Your" show.
                    Well, I want a palimony agreement
                    and I want it now.

                              ARMAND
                    Well, I don't have a palimony
                    agreement on me now. Is tomorrow
                    all right?

                              ALBERT
                    Don't use that tone to me! That
                    sarcastic, contemptuous tone that
                    means you know everything because
                    you're a man, and I know nothing
                    because I'm a woman.

                              ARMAND
                    You're not a woman.

                              ALBERT
                    Oh! You bastard!

                              AGADOR
                    Take it easy, Armand.

                                                              (CONTINUED)

6.

8   CONTINUED: 2   8

                          ALBERT
                    (to Agador)
               Whatever I am he made me. I was
               adorable once. Young and full of
               hope. Now I'm this short, fat,
               insecure, middle-aged <u>thing</u>.

                          ARMAND
               <u>I</u> made you short?

Cyril races into the apartment and stands gasping in the
doorway.

                          CYRIL
               What do I do?--the number's nearly
               over. Do I send Carmen on for
               Starina?

                          ARMAND
               Yes.

                          ALBERT
               No! How dare you!

                          ARMAND
                    (to Cyril)
               Do it!

Cyril starts out.

                          ALBERT
               No!

Cyril stops.

                          ARMAND
               Cyril!

Cyril starts out.

                          ALBERT
               <u>No</u>!

Cyril stops.

                          ARMAND
               CYRIL!

                          ALBERT
               Please! I'll go on. Don't give my
               number away. I'll be good. You'll
               see.

                                        (CONTINUED)

8 CONTINUED: 3   8

                         ARMAND
                    (to Cyril)
               All right. Put the mambo number on
               and tell Dante and Beatrice to
               stand by with the staircase. Go.

Cyril races out.

                         ALBERT
               My hands are shaking. Agador, I
               need some Pirin tablets. Quickly.

                         ARMAND
               What? What are you taking?

                         AGADOR
                    (taking out two tablets
                     wrapped in Kleenex)
               Here. One before the show and one
               after. But no more.

                         ALBERT
               Thank you, thank you my darling
               Agador. Give me...a moment...

Armand and Agador turn and start out. Albert stuffs a piece
of candy into his mouth as they go out and into...

9 THE LIVING ROOM   9

Armand closes the door behind them, then turns on Agador...

                         ARMAND
               What are you doing? Why are you
               giving him drugs? What the hell
               are Pirin tablets.

                         AGADOR
               They're aspirin. With the "A" and
               the "S" scraped off.

                         ARMAND
               No! My God! What a brilliant
               idea.

10 INT. BEDROOM/DRESSING ROOM - NIGHT   10

Albert is running a razor over his arms. Armand runs
in...stops.

                         ARMAND
               I don't believe this! You're
               shaving your arms now!

                                             (CONTINUED)

                              ALBERT
          I didn't have time to wax.
          Indifference is the most awful
          thing in the world, Armand.
                    (he begins applying
                     mascara)
          I've lost and gained over a hundred
          pounds in the last year...
                    (slapping on make-up)
          I've yo-yo'd from a sixteen to a
          ten to a sixteen--and you've never
          said a word. Not one hint of
          encouragement or validation. If it
          wasn't for the Pirin tablets I
          don't think I could go on.

                              ARMAND
          Albert, I'm going to kill myself if
          you don't finish making up.

                              ALBERT
          You don't love me anymore, Armand.

                              ARMAND
          Oh, shit!

                              ALBERT
          There's a man in your life, isn't
          there? I sense it. And I saw a
          bottle of white wine chilling in
          the refrigerator. I only drink
          red. And so do you.

                              ARMAND
          There's no man. I'm switching to
          white because red has tannins.
          There are 150 people out there
          waiting for you...

          Starina hands Armand an anklet. Armand kneels.

                              ARMAND
                    (fastening the anklet)
          ...waiting to applaud you.   To
          applaud the great Starina.

          Starina suddenly kicks Armand, knocking him flat.

                              ALBERT
          What do you do while I'm onstage?
          Where do you go while I'm killing
          myself onstage?

          Armand begins to struggle up. Starina screams.

                                        (CONTINUED)

                    ALBERT
        Go ahead. Hit me. Go on - that's
        what you want to do, isn't it?
        Well, do it! Hit me! Go on! Go
        ON!

Armand glances, discreetly, at his watch, then strikes out
without aiming. His hand connects vaguely with Albert's
shoulder. Albert screams and falls to the ground as if shot.
Armand holds his hand, wincing in pain.

                    ALBERT
        No more! No more! Please, no...
            (he breaks off; looks up)
        Are you all right?

                    ARMAND
        I hurt my thumb.

                    ALBERT
        Oh, my God, forgive me!

                    ARMAND
        No, no. Forgive me, my little
        roundness, my little teddy bear.

                    ALBERT
        Do you love me? Swear that you
        love me.

                    ARMAND
        Of course I love you.

                    ALBERT
        Don't hurt me.

                    ARMAND
        No.

                    ALBERT
        My king.

                    ARMAND
        My queen.

11   INT. CLUB - THE STAGE - NIGHT   11

Armand's voice comes out of the darkness.

                    ARMAND'S VOICE
        Ladies and gentlemen, the one, the
        only, the incomparable--Starina!

                                        (CONTINUED)

11 CONTINUED:

A single spot hits the bottom rung and then moves up, higher
and higher, until a pair of leopard boots appear, followed by
legs, a pair of leopard gloves, holding a leopard muff, and
then finally Starina's head, wearing a leopard hat.

                    ALBERT
          Hello. I'm just back from
          Safari...
                    (waves muff; points to
                    shoes
          Like him? Oh, don't look at me
          like that. I didn't kill him.
          He died. And left me everything.
                    (off the ladder now)
          Hello, darling. Back again? Oh,
          look at those teeth. You must be a
          Kennedy.
                    (looks out)
          Where are the adorable couple
          who're celebrating their
          anniversary here tonight?
                    (a middle-aged couple
                    raise their hands)
          Mon congrats, you sweeties, and I
          may be celebrating something myself
          soon. I think I've found "the
          one"--and he's not a white
          hunter, or the gorgeous pilot who
          flew me to meet the Sultan of
          Brunei, or even the Sultan of
          Brunei himself, who shall remain
          nameless. He's just a boy who
          works behind the counter of a 7-11
          near the airport...
                    (begins singing)
          "I know this grocery clerk,
          unpre-possessing..."

Armand stands in the wings watching for a few moments as
Albert sings, then begins backing toward the door that leads
upstairs...then turns and bolts for the stairs.

12 INT. ARMAND'S APARTMENT - PATIO   12

Agador, the maid, now wearing a "big hair" red wig, is
on the patio taking down the laundry and lip synching
to Starina's number, which drifts up from downstairs.
Armand rushes in.

                    ARMAND
          Get that laundry down and go get
          the white wine out of the refrig-
          erator and put it in a bucket with
          two glasses and take the night off.

                                        (CONTINUED)

12   CONTINUED: 12

                          AGADOR
            Why do you treat me like a servant.

                          ARMAND
            Because you're my fucking houseman.
            Now hurry!

                          AGADOR
            My father was the shaman of his
            tribe, my mother was a high
            priestess...

                          ARMAND
            Well, then it was pretty dumb of
            them to move to New Jersey.

                          AGADOR
            It was, wasn't it? But they wanted
            me to have a career. When can I
            audition for you again?

                          ARMAND
            When you have talent. Will you
            move! And take off Albert's wig
            or I'll tell him you're wearing it.

                          AGADOR
            And I'll tell him that you're
            seeing someone else while he's on
            stage, you beast.

                          ARMAND
            Go!!

    Agador tosses his head, proudly, and twirls out with the
    laundry.

                          ARMAND
                     (calling after him)
            And don't lock the front door when
            you leave.

    Armand hurries into the bedroom, whips off his jacket and
    begins applying pancake.

13   OMITTED   13

14   EXT. SIDE EXIT TO ARMAND'S APARTMENT   14

    After a moment, Agador slouches out of the door, wearing
    thong sandals and a pouch purse slung over his shoulder.
    He saunters down the street as A TAXI draws up to the
    side entrance... and A YOUNG MAN gets out.

15   INT. THE PATIO - ARMAND   15

make-up completed, hurries out of the bedroom and begins
fussily adjusting the candles...then stops as a voice
behind him says, "Hi."

The young man (VAL) stands silhouetted in the doorway.
Armand rushes to embrace him.

                    ARMAND
          You keep getting better looking.

                    VAL
          Thanks. So do you.

                    ARMAND
          Oh, no. Really? I feel so
          bloated.
                    (glances at his reflec-
                    tion in the glass door)
          Do you really think I look good?

                    VAL
          Primo.

                    ARMAND
          You're sweet. I'm glad you let
          your hair grow. Did you eat?

                    VAL
          I'm fine.

                    ARMAND
          Would you like something to drink?

                    VAL
          Beer if you have it.

                    ARMAND
          I do not. Talk about bloat.
          White wine?

                    VAL
                    (abstractedly)
          Swell.
                    (listening, nervously)
          How long has Albert been on?

                    ARMAND
          He just started and I gave Agador
          the night off so we're all alone.
          As requested. Since when do you
          like beer?

                    VAL
          Look, I have something to tell you.

                    ARMAND
          Yes?

                              (CONTINUED)

                              VAL
          And I don't want you to get...how
          you get.

                            ARMAND
          Oh, my God.

                              VAL
          I'm getting married.
                (there is a pause)
          Hello?

                            ARMAND
          Yes...

                              VAL
          I didn't want to tell you over the
          phone...
                (pours Armand some wine)
          It's a girl. I met her at school.
          A wonderful girl. A really great
          girl... Are you upset?

                            ARMAND
                (drinks his entire glass
                 of wine)
          But let me tell you why...
                (refills the glass)
          First of all, you're only twenty...

                              VAL
          Look, pop, I know I'm young...but
          you've always said I was a very
          level-headed guy. And I am.   I
          have job offers, I know what I want
          my future to be...and I have an
          incredible role model.

                            ARMAND
          Oh, please.

                              VAL
          I do. I'm the only guy in my
          fraternity who doesn't come from a
          broken home.

                            ARMAND
          Stop flattering me. It's cheap.
                (turns away)
          Well... This is...this...time thing
          is a joke, isn't it? Yesterday you
          were this little fat thing in
          diapers, going down that slide with
          your "quack-quack."
                (he smiles)
          Remember Mister Quack-quack?
                            (MORE)

                                              (CONTINUED)

                         ARMAND (cont'd)
                    (Val nods, uncomfortably)
          I think Albert still has it
          somewhere...and today you're
          getting married...

                         VAL
          Is it all right, pop?

                         ARMAND
          Does it matter?

                         VAL
          Yes. I want to hear you say it's
          all right before Albert comes up
          and starts screaming.

                         ARMAND
          Well, I won't. I can't. It's too
          crazy. If you do this, you're on
          your own. Don't come to me, don't
          ask me for anything, I don't want
          anything to do with it.

                         VAL
                    (after a moment)
          Okay. Well...
                    (picks up his jacket)
          Goodbye, pop.

                         ARMAND
          Goodbye. Come here!
                    (embraces him)
          You little fool. As if I would let
          you go.

                         VAL
          Then it's...is it all right?

                         ARMAND
          Yes, yes, it's all right.
                    (he lifts the glass)
          Put down your jacket and let's
          drink a toast to this catastrophe.
                    (looks at Val's anxious
                     face)
          I'm joking. It's all right. It's
          all right, son. What's the young
          lady's name?

                         VAL
          Barbara.

16 INT. KEELEY HOUSE - SOMEWHERE IN OHIO - NIGHT   16

Expensively and carefully furnished. SENATOR KEELEY is
shouting at his daughter (BARBARA). MRS. KEELEY is quickly
closing the doors.

                    SENATOR KEELEY
          Are you crazy? It's out of the
          question. You can't get married!
          You're not even eighteen!

                    MRS. KEELEY
          Who is this boy, Barbie? When was
          the last time you saw him?

                    BARBARA
          Please don't call me Barbie. This
          afternoon. At two o'clock. We've
          been sleeping together for a year.

                    SENATOR KEELEY
          Good God! Has he been tested?

                    MRS. KEELEY
          Kevin!

                    BARBARA
          Yes! And so have I.

Mrs. Keeley screams. They both glance at her in annoyance -
and then resume.

                    SENATOR KEELEY
          Look, this will just have to wait
          until after the election. I can't
          deal with this now.

                    MRS. KEELEY
          Where does this young man come
          from, Barbie..ra? Who is his
          father?

                    BARBARA
               (tensely)
          His father...is in the arts. On
          the council. The Council of
          Cultural Arts.

                    MRS. KEELEY
          Really?

                    SENATOR KEELEY
          The ones that funded the
          Mapplethorpe exhibit?

                    BARBARA
          No, no. Goodness, no. He's a
          cultural attache to Greece.

                                        (CONTINUED)

16 CONTINUED:

                    MRS. KEELEY
          Really?

                    SENATOR KEELEY
          What the hell is that?

                    MRS. KEELEY
          That...that's a diplomatic post,
          isn't it? Almost like an
          ambassador? What does the mother
          do?

                    BARBARA
          She's a...housewife.

                    MRS. KEELEY
          Well, that's really refreshing,
          isn't it, Kevin?

                    SENATOR KEELEY
          I don't want to talk about this
          now.

The telephone RINGS. Barbara snatches it up. Her father
hovers nearby.

                    BARBARA
                (into the phone)
          Hello? ... Yes, I just told them.

17 INT. ARMAND'S APARTMENT   17

Val on the phone, standing next to Armand who is holding a
wine glass.

                    VAL
          Yes, me too. And my father is very
          excited. In fact...

18 INT. KEELEY HOUSE - NIGHT - BARBARA   18

as Barbara listens to Val's voice.

                    VAL'S VOICE
          ...he's holding up his glass to
          toast us...

Senator Keeley goes to a second phone...and presses two
buttons. Val's voice comes on over the phone microphone:

                    VAL'S VOICE
          ...I'll put him on. Pop?

                                        (CONTINUED)

18   CONTINUED: 18

            ARMAND'S VOICE   SENATOR KEELEY
      No, no, no...   I thought his parents
                              were in Greece.

                  BARBARA
          (covering the mouthpiece)
      Dad! Get off the phone!

19   ARMAND'S APARTMENT - NIGHT - ARMAND ON THE PHONE   19

                  ARMAND
      Hello, Barbara? Here's to your
      future.
          (bangs the glass against
           the phone and breaks it)
      Shit! I'm sorry. That wasn't my
      toast. I just broke my glass...

                  BARBARA
      That's all right. It was nice
      talking to you...

20   INT. KEELEY HOUSE - NIGHT   20

                  BARBARA
      ...And we'll talk again soon. Bye.
          (she hangs up)
      How dare you listen in on my
      conversation!

               SENATOR KEELEY
      You said his parents were in
      Greece.

                  BARBARA
      They are.

               SENATOR KEELEY
      You saw this boy at two in the
      afternoon and now he's in Greece
      with his parents?

                  BARBARA
      No. I...Greece? No. They're...
      his parents are back from Greece.
      For the winter. They're at their
      vacation house in...South Beach.

                MRS. KEELEY
      Is that like Palm Beach?

                  BARBARA
      Close. It's about two minutes from
      Fisher Island...where Jeb Bush
      lives.

                       (CONTINUED)

20 CONTINUED: 20

                          MRS. KEELEY
                   (impressed)
              Really?

21 INT. ARMAND'S APARTMENT - PATIO - NIGHT   21

    He is sitting alone on the patio now, looking depressed,
    holding a new glass of wine. The shards of the broken wine
    glass are still on the floor.

    There is the sudden SOUND of applause from below. Armand
    finishes his wine, ignoring the clump of footsteps coming up
    the stairs. After a moment, Albert bursts in.

    He stares at the glass in Armand's hand, then at Val's glass
    on the table next to the empty bottle. He points...

                          ALBERT
              Ah-hah!

                          ARMAND
              Wait...

                          ALBERT
                   (hurling a vase)
              Who is he! Who is he!

                          ARMAND
              Will you stop screaming. It's Val.
              It's Val. He's in his room. Go
              on, check if you don't believe me.

22 CLOSE SHOT - VAL'S FACE   22

    lying on a pillow, surrounded by darkness, the covers pulled
    up to his chin. His eyes are closed, perhaps a shade too
    tightly. A hand comes down and brushes the hair off his
    forehead.

    The ANGLE WIDENS to REVEAL Albert, his face transformed by
    affection, looking down at Val. After a moment, he starts
    out, stops to pick up the clothes strewn on the floor, then
    shaking his head, fondly, tiptoes out.

23 EXT. STREETS OF SOUTH BEACH - DAY   23

    Albert, in mint green slacks, walks down a narrow street
    lined with markets...greeting the merchants as he goes
    from stand to stand, squeezing, smelling, tasting...

                          VOICES
              "We've got some nice lobsters
              today, Albert!"
              "Look at these melons. Perfect!"

                                                    (CONTINUED)

23   CONTINUED: 23

                            ALBERT
                Not ripe. No,no. Too ripe. These
                are nice. I'll take three. Better
                make it six, the piglet is home!

24   OMITTED   24

25   INT. BAKERY - DAY   25

                        BAKERY CLERK
                Would you like the cake delivered?

                            ALBERT
                Yes, please. And don't forget to
                write "To my Piglet, from his
                Auntie" on it.

                        BAKERY CLERK
                You got it.

                            ALBERT
                Thank you. Well, I want to get
                back before he wakes up. I'm just
                going to try this sample. Hmm.
                Chocolate Schneken. A triumph.
                Well, bye bye. Perhaps one more
                schneken. Do you mind?...

26   INT. ARMAND'S KITCHEN - DAY   26

      Agador is at the sink. Armand enters in his dressing gown,
      smoking a cigarette. Agador brings him a cup of coffee.

                            ARMAND
                      (takes a sip)
                What is this? Sludge?

                            AGADOR
                Yes. I thought it would be a nice
                change from coffee.
                      (throatily, in his ear)
                You should have told me you were
                meeting Val last night, you bad
                man. I wouldn't have been so
                sassy.

                            ARMAND
                Will you put some clothes on!

                            AGADOR
                Why won't you let me be in the
                show? Are you afraid of my
                Guatemalanness?

                                        (CONTINUED)

26 CONTINUED: 26

                                    ARMAND
                    Your what?

                                    AGADOR
                    My Guatemalanness. My heat. Are
                    you afraid I'll be too primitive
                    for your little estrogen rockettes?

                                    ARMAND
                    Yes. Right. I'm afraid of your
                    heat.

Albert enters, carrying bags.

                                    ALBERT
                    Yoo-hoo! Here I am! The bag lady!
                    Good morning, Agador.

                                    AGADOR
                    Good morning, Madame.

They kiss.

                                    ALBERT
                    Wash these, will you, Agador?
                    They're delivering the rest around
                    noon. Good morning.
                         (kisses Armand)
                    My God, that beard!

Albert opens the dryer, takes Val's clothes out, and begins
folding them. Agador gives him a cup of coffee.

                                    ALBERT
                    Thank you, dear. Hmm. Turkish
                    coffee. Delicious.
                         (to Armand as he folds)
                    Is Val still asleep? He must be
                    exhausted, poor baby. You should
                    have told me he was coming. I'm so
                    ashamed of the way I acted last
                    night...but how could I know? The
                    truth is you can't stand sharing
                    your son with me. You're always
                    pushing me away. Oh, look at
                    this shirt. It's a rag. No
                    matter how many shirts I send that
                    boy... You look awful. What's
                    wrong?

                                    ARMAND
                    Val is getting married.

                                                        (CONTINUED)

                         ALBERT
          Don't be silly. I got a pork roast
          for dinner. I wanted to get filet
          mignons but they're so expensive.
          What do you mean "married"?

                         ARMAND
          I mean...what do you mean what do I
          mean. I mean "married."

                         ALBERT
          I don't understand.

                         ARMAND
          Yes, you do.

                         ALBERT
                    (screaming)
          No!

                         ARMAND
          Some girl he met at school.

                         ALBERT
          But he's a baby! He's too young!
          He'll ruin his life!

                         ARMAND
          We went through all that. The
          bottom line is he's getting married
          no matter what we say, so the less
          said the better.

                         ALBERT
          Oh, my God...I woke up feeling so
          good and now...all of a sudden, I
          feel...so funny.
                    (he grabs his chest)
          Shhh. Take it easy. Just breathe,
          breathe...

Val enters...looks at Armand...sees Albert.

                         VAL
          Oh. You've heard...

                         ALBERT
          Oh, Vallie! Oh, my God! This is
          such a shock. I'm not saying
          anything--I promised your father--
          but you're only twenty and if you
          throw yourself away on some
          dormitory slut, you'll be sorry for
          the rest of your life. There--
          enough said. No more. That's all.
          Subject closed.
                         (MORE)

                                            (CONTINUED)

26   CONTINUED: 3   26

                              ALBERT (cont'd)
                Well, don't just stand there! Give
                me a kiss! or are you too grown-up
                for that now.

                              VAL
                Hello, Albie.

                              ALBERT
                Oh, Armand, he's going to leave us.
                And we won't have any others.

                              ARMAND
                Not without a miracle.

27   INT. KEELEY DINING ROOM - DAY   27

       Senator and Mrs. Keeley are also eating breakfast...and
       watching the TV.

28   ON THE TELEVISION, TWO HOSTS   28

       sit on either side of Senator Keeley and a white-haired man
       (SENATOR JACKSON). All four men are shouting,
       incomprehensibly.

                              SENATOR JACKSON - ON TV
                         (rising above the others)
                ...when I--and Senator Keeley
                here--founded the Coalition for
                Moral Order, it was to express
                moral rather than political...

             YOUNGER HOST - ON TV   OLDER HOST - ON TV
          Oh, come on. Since   Oh, you come on!
          when do moral views   Since always! Once
          get campaign   the liberals
          contributions?   abolished morality...

                              MRS. KEELEY
                It's a wonderful show.

                              SENATOR KEELEY
                It's the most intelligent show on
                television.

                              SENATOR KEELEY-ON TV
                         (his voice rising again)
                ...I think that what Senator
                Jackson is trying to say is that
                morality is political. Abortion,
                same-sex marriage, contempt for
                family values, pornography--they
                wouldn't exist if politicians
                didn't pass laws to protect them.
                And that's why both houses are now
                Republican...

29   RETURN TO KEELEY DINING ROOM   29

The two hosts begin shouting again. Senator Keeley clicks
off the show and picks up some papers and a tape recorder.

                         MRS. KEELEY
          Bravo. It's a perfect platform.

                       SENATOR KEELEY
          Yes. I'm very glad I got on
          Jackson's bandwagon instead of
          Dole's. Dole is just too...too...

                       MRS. KEELEY
          Dark?

                       SENATOR KEELEY
          Actually, I was going to say
          liberal. But he's dark, too.
               (he makes a note)
          I have to fire this woman...

                       MRS. KEELEY
          You know, this boy that Barbie
          wants to marry...

                       SENATOR KEELEY
             (into a tape recorder)
          Miss Porter, Page two, second
          paragraph is "porno" not
          "pronto"...

                       MRS. KEELEY
          I wonder if he's old money. I
          mean...a cultural attache'...

There is a tap on the door and A MAID enters.

                       MAID
          Your campaign manager is calling.
          He says he's got to talk to you.

Senator Keeley rises and goes out to the phone.

                       SENATOR KEELEY
          Hello, Ben. Ready for what? WHAT?

                       MRS. KEELEY
          What's the matter, Kevin?

                       SENATOR KEELEY
          Jackson is dead.

                       MRS. KEELEY
          Oh my God!

                                     (CONTINUED)

29 CONTINUED: 29

                              SENATOR KEELEY
                         (listens, then...)
                    He died in bed. ... Whose bed?...
                         (listens...)
                    A prostitute...

                              MRS. KEELEY
                    No!

                              SENATOR KEELEY
                         (listens)
                    And a minor...
                         (listens)
                    And black!

                              MRS. KEELEY
                    What?

                              SENATOR KEELEY
                    A prostitute ... minor ... black.
                         (he hangs up on the still
                          ranting voice)
                    I don't believe this. I don't
                    fucking believe this! I'm
                    ruined.

                              MRS. KEELEY
                    Why? You're not responsible. You
                    can't be held responsible for
                    Senator Jackson's private life.

                              SENATOR KEELEY
                    Louise, I'm the vice president of
                    the Coalition for Moral Order, and
                    my co-founder has just died in bed
                    with an under-aged black whore.
                    Just wait until the media gets hold
                    of this! ... I could really use a
                    piece of candy.

30 CLOSE SHOT - A SCRAPBOOK   30

    the pages being slowly turned. Pictures of Val as a baby,
    then as a young boy, then an adolescent, posing with Armand
    and Albert, with other friends, a dog...

    OVER THE SHOT we hear the soft, steady SOUND of weeping...
    and piano chords.

                              ARMAND'S VOICE
                    You're driving me crazy, Albert.

    The ANGLE WIDENS to REVEAL Albert sitting on the couch in the
    living room, looking at the scrapbook, an ancient rubber duck
    clutched in one hand. Armand is at the piano, working on a
    tune.

                                                           (CONTINUED)

30   CONTINUED: 30

                         ALBERT
              My baby.
                   (he weeps, quietly)

31   CLOSE SHOT: A TELEVISION SCREEN   31

      A YOUNG BLACK GIRL is speaking:

                         BLACK GIRL - ON TV
              He looked kinda funny but he was
              smilin' so I didn't worry...

                         VOICE - ON TV
              Senator Jackson's last words!
              Tonight--on Inside Edition!

                         MRS. KEELEY'S VOICE
              How do they get them on so quickly.

                         SENATOR KEELEY'S VOICE
              They pay.

      The ANGLE WIDENS to REVEAL...

32   THE KEELEY DINING ROOM   32

      Senator and Mrs. Keeley sitting in front of the television,
      their faces blank with shock.

                         MRS. KEELEY
              They're not mentioning you much.

                         SENATOR KEELEY
                   (his mouth full of candy)
              It's early.

32A   EXT. WIDE SHOT - MIAMI - DAY   32A

      There is a beat...and then a shriek over the shot:

                         ALBERT'S VOICE
              Oh, no! They wrote Uncle!

33   INT. ARMAND'S - KITCHEN - DAY   33

      Armand stands staring down at a newly opened cakebox.

                         ALBERT
              I told them "Auntie"! Uncle! He
              won't know who "uncle" is!

                                              (CONTINUED)

33 CONTINUED: 33

                          ARMAND
                    (calmly measuring
                     ingredients into a bowl)
               He'll probably eat half the cake
               before he looks at it. He's just
               like you.

                          ALBERT
               Yes, the piglet.
                    (he smiles; then suddenly
                     frowns)
               We'll have to completely redecorate
               his room, you know. We can't put a
               married couple in a room that looks
               like a bulletin board. Plus there
               has to be room for the grand-
               children! So there goes your den.

                          ARMAND
               Someone's feeling better.

                          ALBERT
               Well, grandchildren... Oh, I can
               just see you as a grandfather!
               Pushing the carriage, gold chains
               clinking, chest hair dyed...

                          ARMAND
                    (a tiny smile)
               Not a bad sight, is it? Don't stir
               that. It's the marinade. Go get
               ready for rehearsal. Go on.

                          ALBERT
               You never let me help you cook.

                          ARMAND
               Go, go, go. And I'll meet you
               downstairs...grandma.

34 EXT. KEELEY HOUSE - DAY   34

    It is surrounded by television trucks, TV and print
    reporters, cameras.

    A small movement in an upstairs window catches everyone's
    attention.

35 INT. FRONT WINDOW - KEELEY HOUSE - MRS. KEELEY   35

    as she steps quickly back, closing the drapes. Barbara
    enters.

                          BARBARA
               Where's dad?

                                              (CONTINUED)

                    MRS. KEELEY
          He snuck out this morning to meet
          with his advisors. They refused to
          come here.

                    BARBARA
          Mom...

                    MRS. KEELEY
          I should never have let him go.
          How will he get back in.

                    BARBARA
          Mom...I have to tell you
          something...about Val's parents.

                    MRS. KEELEY
          They can't blame us for this. Eli
          Jackson was a common redneck and we
          had nothing to do with him,
          socially. They understand that,
          don't they?
               (Barbara nods, miserably)
          Thank God they're not snobs.

Senator Keeley suddenly appears at the back window clinging
to a branch. He taps on the pane. His face is dirty. His
jacket crushed. Mrs. Keeley and Barbara rush to him.

                    MRS. KEELEY
          What are you doing here?

                    SENATOR KEELEY
          I came through the orchard and over
          the top of the barn.

                    MRS. KEELEY
          But it's so dangerous! You could
          have fallen!

                    SENATOR KEELEY
          I did!

They pull him over the sill.

                    SENATOR KEELEY
          Don't let the ladder drop. We may
          need it. I'm just a wreck! This
          is all anyone can talk about.

                    MRS. KEELEY
          Kevin...if we can manage it...there
          may be a solution.

                    SENATOR KEELEY
          What? Death? It didn't work for
          Jackson.

                              MRS. KEELEY
          What about a wedding.   A big white
          wedding.

                              SENATOR KEELEY
          What do you mean?   What wedding?
          Who's getting married? ...   No!

                              MRS. KEELEY
          Why not?   It will restore your
          image.   A wedding is hope...a white
          wedding is morality and family and
          tradition.   And this would be such
          a special marriage, the son of a
          cultural attache--a kind of
          diplomat, actually--who doesn't
          look down on us because of Senator
          Jackson, who's willing to join our
          family.   There's the cover of
          People and Time and Newsweek--right
          there!   Love and optimism versus
          cynicism and sex.   It will be an
          affirmation.   If necessary we'll
          get the Pope's blessing.   It's not
          hard.

                              SENATOR KEELEY
          I know.   But he's too
          controversial.   Billy Graham...?
          No, too liberal.

                              BARBARA
          Now wait a minute...

                              MRS. KEELEY
          Listen, Barbara, you have three and
          a half years till you're twenty-one
          and you want to get married now.
          Don't be a nitwit.

                              SENATOR KEELEY
          Where's the candy?

                              MRS. KEELEY
          You've had enough candy.
               (turning to Barbara)
          This boy, what's his father's name?

                              BARBARA
          Armand...
               (she swallows)
          ...Coleman.

                              MRS. KEELEY
          Really?   I wonder if they're
          related to Bobo and Tish Coleman.
          Are they from Boston?

                                        (CONTINUED)

29.

35	CONTINUED:	3								35

>						BARBARA
>			I don't think so.

>						MRS. KEELEY
>			I think we should go down to South
>			Beach and meet them, immediately.
>			We can have dinner with them and
>			spend the night with the Bushes.
>					(her eyes glow)
>			Mr. and Mrs. Armand Coleman of
>			Greece and South Beach.

36	INT. THE BIRDCAGE - DAY							36

Albert is in full costume, rehearsing Armand's new song,
while a second performer (CELSIUS) dances around him in
tights and a sleeveless T. Cyril plays the piano. Armand
watches from the house.

Celsius does a bump and grind...then peers over his shoulder
and winks. Albert breaks off.

>						ALBERT
>			Well, this is impossible. Either
>			I'm an artist or I'm just some
>			cheap drag queen playing it
>			straight so he can get laughs.

>						ARMAND
>			Let's just try and get through
>			it...

>						ALBERT
>			You always ask so much of me, I
>			have to understand every nuance of
>			a song, I have to rehearse in full
>			costume. But everyone else can
>			just "get through it." I
>			mean...he's chewing gum!

>						CELSIUS
>			Chewing gum helps me think.

>						ALBERT
>			Sweetie, you're wasting your gum.

>						ARMAND
>			All right, let's take it from the
>			top, no more talk...from anyone.

Albert begins the song again. Val enters.

>						VAL
>			Pop, I have to talk to you.

(CONTINUED)

                          ARMAND
          Shh. Sit down.

                            VAL
          It's important.

                          ARMAND
          Wait! Can't you see he's
          rehearsing?

                          ALBERT
          Armand, did you see what he did?
          Hello, Vallie, darling.

                          ARMAND
          Let's keep going. What did Celsius
          do?

                          ALBERT
          He blew a bubble with his gum.
          While I was singing! He can't do
          that while I'm singing.
               (cries)

                          ARMAND
          Celsius, look...this may be a drag
          show but it still has to be a good
          drag show, if possible--a great
          drag show...

                          ALBERT
          Yes! And just because you're
          eighteen and hung doesn't mean
          you're qualified...

                          ARMAND
          Let me do this, Albert.
               (to Celsius)
          This is a complex number. Full of
          mythic themes. You were invented
          by the woman who's singing, you're
          her fantasy, this gorgeous fantasy,
          free and arrogant...and then,
          suddenly, you, the fantasy, see
          her, your inventor--and she becomes
          your fantasy.

                          CELSIUS
          I don't think I get it.

                          ALBERT
          Try more gum.

                          ARMAND
          Albert! Well, you have to explore
          it, Celsius.
               (MORE)

(CONTINUED)

36 CONTINUED: 2   36

                              ARMAND (cont'd)
            But start with the premise that,
            when you see this stunning,
            smoldering creature - she
            transcends your desire to chew -
            she electrifies you, something
            begins in your pelvis that travels
            straight to your heart - but hit
            the pelvis.

                              CELSIUS
            But what do I do? I don't want
            to just stand here like an
            object.

                              ARMAND
            Do this! 5, 6, 7, 8!
                 (he dances)
            And this! Do a stunning
            eclectic, celebration of dance...
                 (dances; to Albert)
            ...and you, of course, sing...
                 (he dances on...and on)

                              VAL
            Pop!

                              ARMAND
            Coming. All right. Try it again.
            I'll be right back.
                 (he rises)

37 INT. THE BIRDCAGE - DAY - STAIRWAY   37

Armand and Val head up the stairs.

                              ARMAND
            Well?

                              VAL
            Barbara is coming with her parents.

                              ARMAND
                 (he stops)
            When?

                              VAL
            They'll be here tomorrow.

                              ARMAND
            Well, that's plenty of time. Is
            that what you interrupted me for?

                              VAL
            No. There's more. Please, keep
            going.

They continue up the stairs.

38   INT. APARTMENT - DAY   38

          Armand and Val enter. Val goes straight for the bar.

                              VAL
                    Wine?

                              ARMAND
                    No. Hurry. Let's hear it.

                              VAL
                    I think I'll have some.
                         (filling a glass)
                    Barbara's father is a conservative
                    Senator and he's running for
                    re-election, and she told him that
                    you were the Cultural Attache to
                    Greece and Albert was a housewife.
                         (he gulps down the wine)

                              ARMAND
                    What?

                              VAL
                    She had to, Pop. He's a founder of
                    the Coalition for Moral Order.

                              ARMAND
                    I don't care who he is. I don't
                    want to be someone else. Do you
                    want me to be someone else?

                              VAL
                    No, of course not. And neither
                    does Barbara, but her father
                    ...Pop, her father is Kevin Keeley.

                              ARMAND
                    Who's Kevin Keeley?

                              VAL
                         (he stares at him)
                    Do you ever read the newspapers?

                              ARMAND
                    Of course. Variety, The Star, the
                    Arts and Leisure section of the New
                    York Times... Why? Is there
                    something I don't know? You're not
                    marrying some Nazi, are you?

                              VAL
                    No, no. He's just...a
                    conservative...like half of
                    America, and I'm not marrying him,
                    I'm marrying Barbara. And I need
                    your help.

                                             (CONTINUED)

                          ARMAND
          Not for this.

                          VAL
          You've done it before.

                          ARMAND
          What? Lied about who I am? Never.

                          VAL
          Do you remember my first day at
          Edison Park? What you told me?

                          ARMAND
          No.

                          VAL
          You said if Miss Donovan asked me
          what you do for a living, I should
          say you're a businessman.

                          ARMAND
               (after a moment)
          Yes, I did. Because you were a
          baby and Miss Donovan was a
          small-minded idiot and I didn't
          want you to get hurt. But it's
          different now. You're a man.

                          VAL
          But I can still get hurt.
               (he waits)
          Pop, it would mean everything to me
          if you would help us. Just for one
          night...

                          ARMAND
               (there is a pause)
          Well, this is insane! What am I
          supposed to do? Close the club and
          pretend I'm a cultural attache?
          Whatever the hell that is? Make
          Albert into a housewife?

                          VAL
          You'd have to send Albert away for
          a few days. We'll never get him
          past the Keeleys.

                          ARMAND
          Are you crazy? Albert? You try
          sending Albert away.

                          VAL
          And you'll have to get rid of a few
          things around here...

                                        (CONTINUED)

38 CONTINUED: 2   38

                         ARMAND
             What things?

                         VAL
                    (pointing to gold phallus
                     on Armand's chain)
             That, for example.
                    (walking to large nude
                     Greek statue)
             And this -

                         ARMAND
             The Greek? But that's art!

Val points to a primitive sculpture with a large phallus.

                         VAL
             And that.

Armand puts his hand on the sculpture's erect penis and
gently rotates the sculpture so that it's facing the wall.

                         ARMAND
             Is that better?

                         VAL
             No. Look...it's not just one or
             two things...it's everything. I
             mean, you'd have to tone it all
             down, make it more like...other
             people's homes...

                         ARMAND
             So we need a total redecoration
             now? To make us more like other
             people...

                         VAL
             And you have to try to...you know,
             to be...a little less obvious...
             change your mannerisms a little.

                         ARMAND
             What do you mean? I'm obvious?

                         VAL
             Pop...

Val walks over to Armand and runs his fingers down his cheek,
then smears the make-up from his fingertips onto the wall
behind him.

                         ARMAND
             Val, I just had the walls sponge
             painted.

A KNOCK at the door. Cyril sticks his head in.

                                              (CONTINUED)

35.

38 CONTINUED: 4   38

                          CYRIL
            You better get downstairs. She's
            trying to take his chewing gum
            away.

                          ARMAND
            I'll be right there.
                    (to Val)
            Yes, I use foundation. Yes, I live
            with a man. Yes, I'm a middle-aged
            fag. But I know who I am. It's
            taken me twenty years to get here,
            Val, and I'm not going to let some
            idiot Senator destroy it. Fuck the
            Senator! I don't give a damn what
            he thinks.

39 EXT. KEELEY HOUSE - NIGHT   39

    Camera trucks are parked on the street. Outside the wrought
    iron gates, Reporters, Camera crews, lights, Newsmen, all are
    waiting. As the CAMERA PANS, we hear local Newscasters:

                          NEWSPERSON #1
            ...still outside the home of
            Senator Kevin Keeley, co-founder of
            the Coalition for Moral Order...

                          NEWSPERSON #2
            ...waiting for Senator Jackson's
            close friend and colleague, Senator
            Kevin Keeley...

                          NEWSPERSON #3
            ...no sign of Keeley, although an
            earlier report placed him at the
            home of Senator Robert Dole this
            morning...

40 ANGLE - A WEARY OVERWEIGHT REPORTER   40

    HARRY RADMAN is leaning against a tree. He straightens as he
    sees a CHAUFFEUR carrying a suitcase and heading for the
    garage.

    Radman looks quickly around, then steps up to the gate,
    and holds up a wad of bills. The Chauffeur sees the bills,
    glances around...then comes up to the gate.

                          HARRY RADMAN
                    (softly; flashing the
                     bills)
            Where are you driving him?

                                              (CONTINUED)

40 CONTINUED: 40

                          CHAUFFEUR
                   (studies the bills in
                    Radman's hand)
                South Beach, Florida.

Radman hands him the bills. The Chauffeur moves off.

41 CLOSE SHOT - JAY LENO ON TELEVISION   41

                       JAY LENO - ON TV
                   (his face is grave)
                There have been a lot of tasteless
                jokes about the death of Senator
                Eli Jackson...
                   (he suddenly grins)
                ...and now here's another one!

                        VOICE - ON TV
                Tonight on Jay Leno! Jay's guests,
                Michael Huffington and Madonna!

42 There is a click and the set goes to black.   42

                        SENATOR KEELEY (V.O.)
                This is unbearable.

The ANGLE WIDENS to REVEAL...

THE KEELEY BEDROOM

Senator Keeley rises, goes to the window and opens it.
Mrs. Keeley, who has just finished packing a small
overnight case, looks up and screams.

                        MRS. KEELEY
                Kevin, no!

                        SENATOR KEELEY
                Shh. I'm just going down the
                ladder. I can't face the press
                tonight. Tell the chauffeur to
                come around and stop outside the
                orchard.

                        MRS. KEELEY
                   (grabbing him)
                You can't do that. I don't want to
                go out there alone.

                        SENATOR KEELEY
                You won't be alone, you'll have
                Barbara. It's not <u>you</u> they're
                after, Louise...

Barbara comes in. Sees her parents grappling at the window.

                                              (CONTINUED)

42   CONTINUED: 42

                              BARBARA
                         (screaming)
                    Daddy!

                         SENATOR KEELEY
                    Shut up! I'm just trying to get
                    out the back way.

                         MRS. KEELEY
                    Didn't we decide that you were
                    going to announce Barbara's wedding
                    to the Coleman boy?

                         SENATOR KEELEY
                    Not before we meet them. What if
                    they change their minds? Now let
                    go of my coat. I'll meet you in
                    the car.

He puts a leg over the sill and starts down the ladder.

43   EXT. KEELEY GARDEN - NIGHT - SENATOR KEELEY   43

making his way laboriously down the first two rungs.
Suddenly, lights go on. The Senator turns his head and looks
down.

Below him are two Camera Crews, Newscasters, and four or five
Reporters. Senator Keeley clings to the ladder, frozen, like
a rabbit in the headlights. A boom mike appears in the air.

                         NEWSPERSON #1
                         (into camera)
                    ...and--yes. It's Senator Keeley,
                    just leaving his house.
                         (calling up)
                    Senator Keeley, Senator Keeley...

          NEWSPERSON #1   NEWSPERSON #2
     Senator Keeley, do   Senator Keeley,
     you think this will   what's the future of
     cost you votes?   the Coalition for
                                      Moral Order now?

          NEWSPERSON #3   NEWSPERSON #4
     Senator Keeley, what   Senator Keeley, what
     happened at this   about the rumors that
     morning's meeting   Senator Jackson was
     with Senator Dole...   on Lithium...

As the questions proceed, more Newsmen and cameras appear
around the back, climbing over the fence, drawn by the lights
and voices. They pay no attention to the fact that the
Senator is on a ladder.

                                                   (CONTINUED)

43   CONTINUED: 43

                    SENATOR KEELEY
          Gentlemen...and ladies... I am, as
          are all my colleagues, Republican
          and Democrat, liberal and
          conservative alike, stunned and
          saddened by the circumstances
          surrounding the death of Senator
          Jackson...as well as the death
          itself. My family and I are
          leaving town for a few days...for
          reasons I cannot...to plan an
          event...an event which I cannot...
          which may perhaps heal some of
          the...the bad...things...that
          Senator Jackson's demise has made
          us...uh...all feel.

                    NEWSPEOPLE
          "What's the event?"
          "Will you be back in time to attend
          Senator Jackson's funeral?"
          "What's the event, Senator?"
          "Senator Keeley..."

                    HARRY RADMAN
               (above the others)
          Where are you and your family
          going, Senator Keeley?

                    SENATOR KEELEY
          Where? To our...farm. And that's
          all I'm going to say for now.

44   ANGLE - HARRY RADMAN   44

     The beginning of a smile on his jowly face.

45   INT. THE BIRDCAGE - NIGHT   45

     The waiters are just finishing the table set-ups. Albert, in
     full costume and make-up, is doing a sound check with
     Celsius. An occasional performer flits across the stage in
     back of them.

     Armand stands, moodily, drinking a glass of wine.

46   INT. VAL'S BEDROOM - NIGHT - VAL   46

     sitting on the edge of the bed, staring hopelessly at the
     floor. Through the door we hear the faint sound of the music
     downstairs.

     There is the sudden harsh sound of footsteps in the other
     room, then Armand's voice...

                                                  (CONTINUED)

46 CONTINUED: 46

                              ARMAND'S VOICE
                    Agador! Goddamnit!

                              AGADOR'S VOICE
                    What did I do?

                              ARMAND'S VOICE
                    We're redoing the apartment for
                    tomorrow night. God<u>damn</u> it!

Val sits up, slowly, his eyes brightening.

47 INT. LIVING ROOM - NIGHT - ARMAND, AGADOR   47

Armand moves around the room, agitatedly.

                              AGADOR
                    This is for the in-laws, right?

                              ARMAND
                    Right. Get rid of everything over
                    the top. And get yourself a
                    uniform. You'll have to dress like
                    a butler.

                              AGADOR
                    I'll look like a fag.

                              ARMAND
                    Maybe. But you'll look like a fag
                    in a uniform.
                         (he sighs)
                    You'll start first thing in the
                    morning. I'll get Albert out of
                    the house early...and tell him he
                    has to leave for a few days...

                              AGADOR
                         (into his own problem)
                    Where'm I going to get a uniform...

                              ARMAND
                    Oh, <u>God</u>!...this will be hard...

                              AGADOR
                    Oh, God, so much to do...

                              VAL
                    Pop...

Armand turns. Val stands in the doorway.

                              VAL
                    Thanks.

                              ARMAND
                    Do me a favor, Val - don't talk to
                    me for a while.

48   EXT. THE STARLIT SKY   48

as it DISSOLVES to DAWN...

The CAMERA pans down to a...

BLACK LINCOLN - ON THE HIGHWAY - NIGHT - DRIVING

The Keeleys sit crammed in back. The Chauffeur is driving.

                    MRS. KEELEY
          Kevin, please let's charter a
          plane.

                    SENATOR KEELEY
          No. We can't get out of this car.
          The minute we get out of this car
          we'll be spotted.

The Chauffeur lifts his eyes to the rear view mirror...where
a SILVER ESCORT is reflected.

49   SILVER ESCORT - ON THE HIGHWAY - NIGHT   49

Radman is driving. Next to him is a second man (THE
PHOTOGRAPHER) with a camera in his lap.

50   EXT. BEACH - MORNING   50

MODELS, GAY MEN, A FEW LESBIANS, ATTRACTIVE TOURISTS...all
out in the morning sun.

Albert and Armand sit on the sand. Armand wears a safari cap
and glasses. Albert wears a straw sombrero, glasses and long
sleeves. They are sitting under an umbrella.

                    ALBERT
          Oh, how I love the sun.

                    ARMAND
          Yes. It's glorious, isn't it? You
          know, you could use some sun...
          take a few days off...you look
          tired.

                    ALBERT
          What do you mean?

                    ARMAND
          I... Nothing.

51   INT. ARMAND'S APARTMENT - DAY   51

Cyril is there, along with the "girls" from the show. One
"girl" is carrying out Albert's wigs. Two others are taking
down an enormous oil painting of a satyr.

                                                  (CONTINUED)

51 CONTINUED: 51

Cyril is pinning up Agador's trousers.

                         AGADOR
               Not too short. I want that
               Armani "buckle" in front...

                         VAL
                  (running in with a
                   magazine)
               Who put Playboy in the bathroom?

                         GIRL
               Leave it. It's what they read.

                         VAL
               Look, don't add anything. Just
               subtract. And hurry. This place
               has got to look respectable by six.

52 EXT. A STREET IN SOUTH BEACH - DAY   52

Armand hurries along beside Albert.

                         ALBERT
               But you must have meant something.

                         ARMAND
               I didn't. I swear. I just meant
               you look tired.

                         ALBERT
               That means "old." "You look tired"
               means you look old. And "you look
               rested" means you've had collagen.

                         ARMAND
               No, no. You look wonderful. Too
               good to waste indoors. Let's...
               let's window shop.

                         ALBERT
               No, thank you. I want to go home.

                         ARMAND
               On a day like this? Nonsense.
               Come on, I'll buy you anything you
               want.

                         ALBERT
               Well...I'll have to change my
               shoes.

                         ARMAND
               I'll buy you a pair.

                                        (CONTINUED)

52 CONTINUED: 52

                         ALBERT
            I have no peds. Armand, why can't
            we go home? What's going on?

                         ARMAND
            Nothing. I...nothing.

Albert turns the corner and starts toward the entrance.
Armand suddenly cries out. Albert turns.

                         ARMAND
            I...I've hurt my...thing...ankle...

                         ALBERT
            Your what?

                         ARMAND
            My ankle. I don't think I can make
            it upstairs.

                         ALBERT
            Do you want to wait here and I'll
            bring some ice down?

                         ARMAND
            No, I...just... No...

53 INT. ARMAND'S APARTMENT - DAY   53

It has progressed. Many of the ornate touches are gone along
with much of the Greek art. Two "girls" come in the front
door carrying a large moose head.

                         VAL
            What's that?

                         GIRL
            It's from the antique shop across
            the street. Too butch?

                         VAL
            Don't add!

Through the door, we suddenly hear Albert's voice. Everyone
freezes.

                         ALBERT'S VOICE
            ...you're blocking my way.

                         ARMAND'S VOICE
            I'm sorry. I can't walk any
            faster...

                         VAL
            Put the moose head in my room! In
            my room!

                                              (CONTINUED)

53 CONTINUED: 53

The two "girls" fly into the den...as everyone else runs for
the door leading to the club. The sound of their footsteps
echoes through the apartment as they clamber down the back
stairs.

54 INT. FRONT STAIRS - DAY   54

Armand and Albert walking up. Armand is leaning on Albert.

                       ARMAND
          ...I really think a doctor...

                       ALBERT
        Don't be silly.
          (he whisks up Armand's
          pant leg)
        It isn't even swollen. Here...

Albert flings open the door to the apartment.

55 INT. ARMAND'S APARTMENT - DAY   55

Only Val is there, pressed into a corner.

                       ALBERT
        Sit down on the --
          (he screams)

                     ARMAND
        What is it?

                     ALBERT
        We've been robbed!

                     VAL
        No, Albie, we...I've just taken a
        few things out...they'll all be in
        place by the time you get back.

                     ALBERT
        Back? Where am I going?

                     VAL
          (to Armand)
        You didn't tell him?

                     ALBERT
        What? Tell me what?

                     ARMAND
          (taking a deep breath)
         Val's fiancee is coming tonight--
        with her parents. And we...we
        thought...it would be better if you
        weren't here.

                                     (CONTINUED)

55 CONTINUED: 55

                              ALBERT
                         (there is a pause)
                    I see.
                         (he sits)
                    I see.

                              VAL
                    It's just for tonight...

                              ALBERT
                    I understand. It's just while
                    people are here. It's all right,
                    my darling. It's nothing. It's
                    painful, but it's not important.
                    I'm leaving. The monster. The
                    monster is leaving. You're safe.

          Albert rises and walks out the front door.

                              ARMAND
                         (to Val)
                    That went well.

          He runs out after Albert. Val stands staring after them.
          Agador and the two "girls" with the moose head come out of
          the den. No one speaks.

56 EXT. OUTDOOR CAFE - DAY - ALBERT   56

          running past it as Armand follows. The Customers watch,
          riveted.

                              ARMAND
                         (panting)
                    Albert ...will you listen!

                              ALBERT
                    Go away! I hate you! I never want
                    to see you again!
                         (he suddenly sobs)
                    My heart is breaking.

                              ARMAND
                    Oh, God. Please. Don't cry. It's
                    all right. You can stay.

                              ALBERT
                    No. I don't want to stay where I'm
                    not wanted, where I can be thrown
                    out on a whim, without legal
                    rights...

                              ARMAND
                    I have the palimony papers at home.

                                                    (CONTINUED)

                    ALBERT
        You're lying again.
            (he staggers)
        This is too much for me. Too much
        ugliness, too much pain. Here,
        feel my pulse. Am I all right?

                    ARMAND
           (soothingly)
        My goodness. It's _very_ fast.
        Let's get you out of the sun...

Armand leads him toward one of the umbrella-topped tables. A
WAITER hurries over.

                    ARMAND
        Water. Right away.

                    WAITER
        Right away.

The Waiter scoots off as Armand slides a chair under Albert.

                    ALBERT
        It's the end. It's the end, I know
        it is.

                    ARMAND
        Sit down. Breathe, breathe...

The Waiter flies back, carrying a pitcher and two glasses.

                    ARMAND
        Thank you. And the usual.

                    WAITER
        Right away, Senor Goldman.

The Waiter flies off again and Armand dips a napkin into his
water and holds it on the back of Albert's neck.

                    ALBERT
        Thank you. That's better.

                    ARMAND
        This is not because of _you_. This
        is because this girl's parents are
        assholes. Val is _crazy_ about you.
           (wipes Albert's face with
            a freshly dipped napkin)

                    ALBERT
        Is he? Oh that helps. Oh, you're
        sweet. That water is so cool.
           (he sips his water)
               (MORE)

(CONTINUED)

                        ALBERT (cont'd)
Maybe...maybe it is too much to
introduce me as his mother on the
first visit. Could you tell them
I was a relative who dropped in?
Val's uncle? Uncle Al?

                        ARMAND
What's the point? Then you'll be
Val's gay uncle Al.

                        ALBERT
I could play it straight.

                        ARMAND
Oh, please. Look at you. Look at
how you're holding your glass.
Look at your posture. Look at your
pinky.

                        ALBERT
           (curling his pinky down)
And what about you? You're
obviously not a cultural--whatever
it is. You've never been to a
museum and you eat like a pig.

                        ARMAND
Albert, these people are right wing
conservatives. They don't care if
you're a pig. They just care if
you're a fag.

The Waiter whips over with two club sandwiches.

                        WAITER
Right away.

Albert sits staring at the club sandwich, motionless, his
eyes down, his shoulders sagging. There is a pause.

                        ARMAND
Oh, fuck 'em! Of course, you can
pass as an uncle. You're a great
performer. And I'm a great
director! Together we can
do...almost anything.

                        ALBERT
Oh, Armand. Really?

                        ARMAND
Absolutely. We have five hours.
Let's get started. First--your
pinky. It's up again. Get it
down. And sit up straight!
           (he slaps his back)

                                              (CONTINUED)

56   CONTINUED: 3   56

                                    ALBERT
                    Oh!--my God! Are you crazy! What
                    are you doing?

                                    ARMAND
                    Stop whining. I'm teaching you to
                    be a man. Now this is a dinner
                    party so let's work with the food.
                    Spread some mustard on that bread.
                    Not with the spoon. Don't dribble
                    little dots of mustard on. Take
                    the knife and smear. Men smear.
                    And get that goddamned pinky down.
                    Your fingers are iron. Stop
                    trembling. Hold the knife boldly.
                    With strength.

                                    ALBERT
                               (hysterically)
                    Oh, God! I've pierced the toast!

                                    ARMAND
                    So what? The important thing is
                    not to go to pieces when that
                    happens. React the way a man
                    would. Calmly. Just say to
                    yourself, "Albert, you pierced the
                    toast. So what? Your life isn't
                    over." Try another one.

                                    ALBERT
                    You're right, you're right.
                    There's no need to get hysterical.
                    All I have to remember is that I
                    can always get more toast.

                                    ARMAND
                    That's the spirit. Now let's see
                    you walk.

                                    ALBERT
                    Holding the sandwich?

                                    ARMAND
                    It...doesn't matter. Just walk.

After a moment of indecision, Albert puts the sandwich down,
rises, and walks.

                                    ALBERT
                    Too swishy?

                                    ARMAND
                               (after a moment)
                    Let me give you an image. A
                    cliche' but an image. John Wayne.

                                                        (CONTINUED)

56   CONTINUED: 4   56

                              ALBERT
                    John Wayne?

                              ARMAND
                    You're a fan. He had a very
                    distinctive walk, very easy to
                    imitate, and if <u>anyone</u> was a
                    man...Try it. Just get off your
                    horse and head for the saloon.
                    Come on.

          Albert begins the John Wayne walk; knees together, hips
          shifting.

                              ALBERT
                    No good?

                              ARMAND
                    Actually...it's perfect. I just
                    never realized John Wayne walked
                    like that.

57   EXT. ACCESS ROAD - SENATOR KEELEY'S LINCOLN   57

          The Senator, in hat and dark glasses, is now driving. The
          Chauffeur sits beside him, sleeping. Barbara and Mrs. Keeley
          sit in the back, clutching their safety belts.

          A SIGN on the side of the road says: <u>I-95 SOUTH</u> with an
          arrow pointing left. The Senator swerves left sharply...to a
          chorus of horns.

58   INT./EXT. SILVER ESCORT   58

          The Photographer, who is now driving, screeches to the left
          after the Lincoln. Radman snaps awake.

                              PHOTOGRAPHER
                    This guy is a fucking maniac.

                              HARRY RADMAN
                    Yeah...I wonder what's in South
                    Beach.

59   EXT. A PARK - ARMAND, ALBERT   59

          Armand stands under a tree, pretending to read a newspaper.
          Albert, also carrying a newspaper, lurches toward him, "sees"
          Armand...and holds out his hand.

                              ALBERT
                    Armand Goldman! You old so-and-so.
                    How about those Dolphins?
                              (MORE)

                                                          (CONTINUED)

                         ALBERT (cont'd)
                    (there is a pause)
               Screaming fag?

                         ARMAND
                    (after a moment)
               Stick your hand out sideways, not
               palm down. I'm going to shake it
               not kiss it. And tighten that
               wrist. No, straighten it and
               then tighten it. Better.
                    (he shakes Albert's rigid
                     hand)
               Al! You old so-and-so!

                         ALBERT
               I just said that.

                         ARMAND
               Well, now I'm saying it. Al--you
               old so-and-so! How do you feel
               about that call today; a fourth-
               and-three play from the Dolphins
               with only sixty-four seconds left.

                         ALBERT
               How do you think I feel? Betrayed.
               Bewildered.
                    (a beat)
               Wrong response?

                         ARMAND
               I'm not...sure.
                    (he is sweating)
               Take it from the top.

                         ALBERT
               This is very exciting.

                         ARMAND
               Yes...it is...fella. Damn right.
               Fuckin' A right! Swing that by
               me again, compadre.

Albert begins backing up toward his starting point, crashing
into a man in pink shorts sitting on the grass with a friend.

                         MAN
               Hey!

                         ALBERT
               Oh, sorry.

                         MAN
               Take it easy.

                                              (CONTINUED)

59 CONTINUED: 2   59

                         ARMAND
                    (rising)
          You take it easy, pilgrim.

                          MAN
          Well, he bumped into me.

                         ARMAND
          Well, tough gazongas.

                          MAN
          Why are you being such a prick?

                         ARMAND
          Why are you being such an asshole?

                          MAN
                    (rising; to a very full
                     height)
          Did you just call me an asshole?

                         ARMAND
          No...actually, I was talking to the
          asshole behind you.

60 INT. ARMAND'S APARTMENT - DAY   60

     Armand is lying on the couch. Albert is applying cold
     compresses to his head.

                         ALBERT
          See? The swelling's already gone
          down. It's nothing. You were
          magnificent. Marvelous. Very
          masculine. I'm so proud of you.
          That big idiot looked so ridiculous
          when he sat on you and banged your
          head on the ground. He didn't even
          know how to box.

     Val enters with a towel. Outside we hear Agador's voice
     singing "Vogue" in a high soprano.

                         ALBERT
          Oh, you're a dear, Vallie. I'll go
          get some ice. Be right back, love!
                    (he punches Val, lightly,
                     goes out)

                          VAL
          Can't we hire a straight maid for
          tonight?

                                          (CONTINUED)

                    ARMAND
          There are no straight maids in
          South Beach.
               (he takes the towel)
          And I have more bad news for you.
          I told Albert he could stay.

                    VAL
          What! _Why_?

                    ARMAND
          Why? Because he said his heart was
          breaking. Because he's my friend
          and companion.

                    VAL
          But what...who will we say he is?

                    ARMAND
          Your uncle.

                    VAL
          My...! Well, forget it. We might
          as well forget the whole thing.

                    ARMAND
          Don't be so negative. You're only
          twenty years old. Have some hope.

                    VAL
          About what? I mean, once they see
          you and Albert together... Oh, God,
          what a mess...

                    ARMAND
          What we really need is a woman. We
          could get away with Albert as an
          uncle if we had a woman as a
          mother. Ironic, isn't it? When
          you _need_ a woman...
               (suddenly)
          Why don't I just ask your mother?

Albert appears unseen in the doorway.

                    VAL
          My mother! My mother wouldn't do
          it! ...would she?

                    ARMAND
          How do we know?

                    VAL
          Well, she hasn't seen me in twenty
          years. That's a pretty good
          indication.

                                        (CONTINUED)

60 CONTINUED: 2   60

                          ARMAND
                No, it isn't. Twenty years ago she
                was a young girl...scared, broke...
                But now...

                          ALBERT
                (from the doorway)
                It's very unfair of you to try and
                talk Val into this, Armand. He has
                every reason not to...

                          VAL
                (to Armand)
                You really think she'd do it? Wow.
                (with a touch of awe)
                My mother...

61 INT. KATHARINE ARCHER'S OFFICE   61

Uncluttered, tasteful. KATHARINE ARCHER sits behind a large
glass desk. She is in her 40s--stunning, beautifully
groomed. She is talking into a clear plastic phone.

                          KATHARINE
                Oh, my God! Armand! I don't
                believe it! It's been a hundred
                years. Where are you? ...

62 INT./EXT. A YELLOW CAR - WHIZZING ALONG A FREEWAY   62

Armand, behind the wheel, is talking on a cellular phone.
Albert sits in the passenger seat, arms folded.

                          ARMAND
                On the road. ... I'll be there in
                five minutes. ...me, too. ...Bye.
                (hangs up; to Albert)
                She's going to see me. Why don't I
                drop you off at a cafe. I'll be
                back in fifteen minutes.

                          ALBERT
                That's all right. I'll go up with
                you. I'm sure there's a waiting
                room.

63 INT. OFFICE BUILDING CORRIDOR   63

The entire floor is taken up by the offices of THE ARCHER
SPA. Armand and Albert go through a door that says
KATHARINE ARCHER, PRESIDENT.

64   INT. OUTER OFFICE - ARMAND, ALBERT   64

walk in. A SECRETARY at a white lacquered desk looks up.

>   ARMAND
>   Miss Archer, please. Armand
>   Goldman.

>   SECRETARY
>   Go right in.

65   INT. KATHARINE ARCHER'S OFFICE   65

She rises as Armand enters.

>   KATHARINE
>   Army Goldman.

>   ARMAND
>   Katie Archer.
>   (they smile)
>   Or is it Mrs. something...?

>   KATHARINE
>   No, I'm between husbands. Sit
>   down. My God! I've thought about
>   you so many times...every time I
>   saw an ad for The Birdcage. Are
>   you still with Albert?

>   ARMAND
>   Yes, yes. Still together. And
>   you--you've done very well.

>   KATHARINE
>   Because of you. The money you gave
>   me started this place. You should
>   have gotten stock for it.

>   ARMAND
>   I got Val for it. It was a fair
>   trade.

>   KATHARINE
>   Is he... How is he?

>   ARMAND
>   Fine. He wants to get married.

>   KATHARINE
>   Married! How old is he?

>   ARMAND
>   He's twenty.

>   KATHARINE
>   Twenty... My God, twenty years...

(CONTINUED)

65   CONTINUED:

                             ARMAND
                  And today, for the first time, he
                  <u>really</u> needs you...

66   INT. OFFICE BUILDING - WAITING ROOM - DAY

      Albert is checking his make-up in his compact mirror. The
      Secretary watches him out of the corner of her eye.

      Katharine's voice comes over the INTERCOM.

                        KATHARINE'S VOICE
                  Imelda, cancel my appointments for
                  tonight.

67   INT. KATHARINE'S OFFICE - DAY

      She clicks off the intercom.

                             ARMAND
                  Thank you.

                           KATHARINE
                  It's a pleasure. Really.
                        (she walks to the bar)
                  I normally drink vegetable juice
                  during business hours, but for
                  this--

      She takes out a bottle of champagne and two glasses.

                           KATHARINE
                  --Let's drink to Senator Keeley's
                  daughter and our Val. I'm afraid I
                  haven't done much for him in the
                  last twenty years.

                             ARMAND
                  Don't worry about it. Really.

                           KATHARINE
                  I'm not exactly maternal.

                             ARMAND
                  I am. And Albert is almost a
                  breast.

                           KATHARINE
                  Val was lucky, wasn't he? What
                  time tonight?

                                              (CONTINUED)

                         ARMAND
          Seven o'clock to be safe. We'll do
          a little show for them and then
          send them on their way.
                    (he takes the champagne)

                         KATHARINE
          Do you remember the show we were in
          when we met?

                         ARMAND
          Yes. Very well.

He sings a few phrases. She joins him. He does a few dance
steps, she joins him. Together they reconstruct the routine.

                         ARMAND
          Ah, the life of the gypsy...

                         KATHARINE
                    (as they dance)
          How handsome you were. How
          unavailable. And what a body.

                         ARMAND
          Stop - you're embarrassing me!

                         KATHARINE
          You were so terrified! It was so
          sweet.

                         ARMAND
          I thought I was going to have a
          heart attack. I mean, I walk into
          my room and there's a woman in my
          bed!

                         KATHARINE
          I paid the doorman $20. $20 in
          those days!

                         ARMAND
          And I was so drunk on champagne...
          I thought, "What the hell, why not
          just try it once with a woman and
          see what the straight guys are
          raving about."

                         KATHARINE
          And how long did we last?

                         ARMAND
          I know exactly how long. From 2:30
          to 3:45 a.m. Two times.

68   EXT. REST STOP - BLACK LINCOLN/SILVER ESCORT - PARKED - DAY   68

Barbara sits in the car with the Chauffeur, each wrapped in
his own thoughts. After a moment, Senator and Mrs. Keeley
come out of adjoining restrooms, seconds apart, shaved,
changed and combed for dinner. They climb into the car and
head toward the highway, where a big sign is visible:
WELCOME TO FLORIDA.

The silver Escort follows.

69   INT. VAL'S BEDROOM AND PART OF THE LIVING ROOM   69

Through the open door, we see a few of the "girls" putting
books on shelves. Val stands at the mirror, his hand out.

                    VAL
          Hi. I'm Val. Mrs. Archer, I'm
          Val. Hi. Mom...I'm Val. I'm
          Val...mom... Senator and Mrs.
          Keeley...and Barbara...I'd like you
          to meet my mother...mom... Oh, God,
          please. Let this work out.

70   INT. KATHARINE ARCHER'S WAITING ROOM - ALBERT   70

He looks up at the clock, anxious and impatient...then begins
drumming his fingers on his knee.

71   INT. KATHARINE'S OFFICE - KATHARINE, ARMAND   71

Armand is on the couch now. His jacket off, his shirt damp.
He is on his second glass of champagne. He wipes his face.

                    ARMAND
          Phew. You're in incredible shape.
          And you can still dance.

                    KATHARINE
          So can you, Armand. So can you.
                (dips a napkin in ice,
                 touches it to his face)

                    ARMAND
          Ah, that feels good. Cool.

                    KATHARINE
                (putting her cool hand
                 under his shirt)
          Where did all this hair come from?
          Wasn't your chest smooth?

                    ARMAND
          I shaved it off for the show. I
          wanted to look so young...

                                        (CONTINUED)

71   CONTINUED: 71

                              KATHARINE
                    It's so much nicer this way, so
                    much more masculine. So much hair.
                    Let me touch it. What a beautiful
                    chain. Look how it glitters in
                    that thick, black nest of hair.
                    Unbutton your shirt. I want to
                    stroke your chest, your beautiful,
                    hairy chest...

                              ARMAND
                    Careful with your nails. This
                    shirt is silk organza... Oh!
                    Look, see? You pulled a thread.

The door suddenly flies open and Albert stands there...with
the Secretary behind him. He stares at Armand and Katharine
sprawled across the couch.

                              SECRETARY
                    I'm sorry, Ms. Archer, I couldn't
                    stop him...

Albert turns and goes out.

                              ARMAND
                    Albert!

72   EXT. SOUTH BEACH - DAY   72

Albert runs toward the yellow car, gets in and drives off.

73   INT. ARMAND'S APARTMENT - DAY   73

The room is somber now, almost morose. Agador stands on a
stack of books, putting a huge crucifix above the mantel.
The door opens and Armand runs in.

                              ARMAND
                    Is Albert here?

                              AGADOR
                    No.

                              ARMAND
                    Great. Then he's driving back from
                    Miami at twenty miles an hour with
                    the parking brake on and I had to
                    take the fucking bus!
                            (suddenly seeing the
                             gloomy decor, the cross)
                    Are we crucifying someone tonight?

                                              (CONTINUED)

                              AGADOR
              Do you like it? I traded the moose
              head for it. And they threw in the
              books. It all goes back tomorrow.

Val comes in holding a pile of tabloids, sees Armand, stops.

                              VAL
              Dad! What happened? Did you see
              her? My mother? Is she coming.

                              ARMAND
              Yes...she's coming...

                              VAL
                  (flinging the tabloids
                   into the air)
              Okay!!

                              ALBERT
              Ah, there! You see? It all worked
              out...

They turn. Albert stands in the doorway.

                              ALBERT
              I'm only here to get my toothbrush.
              Agador--will you? It's in the
              usual place.
                  (to Val)
              How I would have loved to have seen
              your children.

                              ARMAND
              Shouldn't you be holding the
              crucifix? It's the prop for
              martyrs.

                              ALBERT
              Oh, yes. Another gibe, another
              joke at my expense. You were
              probably laughing at me with
              Katharine, too. Well, why not?
              I'm not young, I'm not new, and
              everyone laughs at me. I'm quite
              aware of how ridiculous I am. And
              I've been thinking that the only
              solution is to go where nobody is
              ridiculous, where everyone is
              equal. Goodbye, Armand.

                              AGADOR
              Wait!
                  (hands him a toothbrush)
              Here! Please don't go, Miss
              Albert.

                                            (CONTINUED)

                          ALBERT
          My poor Agador. I'm leaving you my
          stereo...my red boots...and my
          wigs. My best wigs. I won't need
          them where I'm going.

                          ARMAND
          All right. I'll bite. Where are
          you going.

                          ALBERT
          To Los Copa.

                          ARMAND
          Los Copa? There isn't anything in
          Los Copa but a cemetery.

                          ALBERT
          I know. That's why I'm packing
          light.

                          ARMAND
          Oh, I see...you're going to the
          cemetery. With your toothbrush.

                          ALBERT
          Goodbye, Armand.
               (he walks out)

                          AGADOR
          Miss Albert!
               (he drops to his knees
                before the crucifix)

                          ARMAND
          Shit!

                          VAL
          It's all right. It will be better
          without an uncle.

                          ARMAND
          Get up, Agador.

                          AGADOR
          I'm praying.

                          ARMAND
          Well, don't. You have to start
          dinner--because I have to go
          after fucking Albert.

He slams out. Val stares at Agador.

                          VAL
          Can you...You can cook, right?

                          AGADOR
          Your father seems to think so.

sits on a bench eating from a bag of chocolate schneken.

Armand pulls up in the car and gets out...then he walks over
to the bench and sits next to Albert.

> ARMAND
> You know, my cemetery is in Key
> Biscayne. It's the prettiest in
> the world. There are lovely trees,
> the sky is blue. There are birds.
> The one at Los Copa is really shit.
> (he leans back)
> What a pain in the ass you are.
> (shakes his head)
> And it's true. You're not young
> and you're not new. And you do
> make people laugh. And me - I'm
> still with you because you make me
> laugh. So you know what I have to
> do? I have to sell my plot in Key
> Biscayne and get a plot beside
> yours in that shithole, Los Copa,
> to make sure I never miss a laugh.
> (taking out a folded
>   sheaf of papers)
> Here.

> ALBERT
> What's this?

> ARMAND
> Read it.

Albert takes the papers, puts on his glasses, and reads.

> ALBERT
> (looks up)
> I don't understand.

> ARMAND
> What's so difficult? It's the
> palimony papers. I told you I had
> them.

> ALBERT
> It says I have the right to give
> you half of everything I own.

> ARMAND
> Yes. I think it will be safer if
> something happens to one of us...

> ALBERT
> But who owns it now?

> ARMAND
> You do.

(CONTINUED)

74 CONTINUED: 74

                          ALBERT
          You've given me the club? And the
          apartment? And everything?

                          ARMAND
          Yes.

                          ALBERT
                 (looks down, cries)
          I don't want it.

                          ARMAND
          Then give me half.

                          ALBERT
          Oh, quick! Give me a pen! I don't
          want all this.

                          ARMAND
                 (handing Albert a pen)
          Here. Sign it. There. We're
          partners. You legally own half my
          life and I legally own half of
          yours.

                          ALBERT
          But half of the club...

                          ARMAND
          Do you think it matters? Take it
          all. I'm fifty years old and
          there's one place in the world I
          call home...and that's because
          you're there. So take it. What
          difference does it make if I let
          you stay or you let me stay...

75 INT. KATHARINE ARCHER'S OFFICE - THE SECRETARY   75

    at her white desk. The phone rings. She picks it up.

                          SECRETARY
          Hello? No, I'm sorry, Mr. Goldman,
          she's left. But she always calls
          in. Yes, I'll give her the
          message. Go ahead.
                 (writes it down)
          "Don't come...".

76 INT. THE YELLOW CAR   76

    as Armand hangs up and reaches for the door.

77   EXT. SOUTH BEACH BUS STOP - ALBERT   77

still seated on the bench, his hands folded, primly in his
lap. He looks up as Armand opens the car door and sticks his
head out.

                         ARMAND
               It's done. Come home.

78   EXT. SENATOR KEELEY'S LINCOLN - DRIVING - DAY   78

The Chauffeur is now at the wheel. Senator Keeley sits
beside him, listening to a VOICE over the car RADIO.

                         RADIO VOICE
               ...and the Reverend Al Sharpton in
               an interview today said that
               Senator Jackson's last words--
               "Your money's on the dresser,
               Chocolate"--were racist and
               demeaning. The prostitute's given
               name is Natumbundra...

                         SENATOR KEELEY
                    (he turns it off; the car
                     swerves briefly)
               That idiot Jackson! Now the blacks
               will start.

                         MRS. KEELEY
               Barbara's wedding will disassociate
               us from all this. Really. The
               Colemans are a perfect family.
               They've never even been divorced,
               have they, Barbara?

                         BARBARA
                    (in a small voice)
               No.

                         MRS. KEELEY
               You see? We're on our way to
               salvation.

The SIGN up ahead says: MIAMI - 80 MILES.

79   CLOSE SHOT - VAL   79

listening in horror to Armand's voice.

                         ARMAND'S VOICE
               ...it was a question of Albert--or
               your mother. So I had to choose...

The ANGLE WIDENS to REVEAL

ARMAND'S LIVING ROOM

Armand is adjusting his tie in a mirror.

                    ARMAND
          ...and I chose Albert. You
          understand that, son...
               (he inspects himself)
          Why can't I get this damned tie
          even! Well, the jacket will cover
          it...
               (buttons jacket)
          I look like my grandfather in this
          suit. He dressed like this in
          every picture. He killed himself
          when he was thirty. Any last
          instructions?

                    VAL
               (dully)
          No. Just...don't talk too much.
          Don't walk unless you have to. And
          try not to gesture. It doesn't
          matter. It won't work.

                    ARMAND
          It <u>will</u>! Don't be so damned
          <u>negative</u>. I think we can pull
          this off...

The bedroom door opens and Albert stands there wearing a
severe dark suit. He walks in and sits down. He doesn't
quite know what to do with himself.

                    ALBERT
          What? No good? Why? I'm dressed
          just the way you are. I took off
          all my rings. I'm not wearing
          make-up. I'm just a "guy."

                    ARMAND
               (points to Albert's
                socks; they are pink)
          What about those?

                    ALBERT
          Oh, those? ...Well, one <u>does</u> want
          a hint of color. Why? What are
          you thinking? You're thinking that
          dressed this way I'm even more
          obvious, aren't you? You hate me.
          I so wanted to help you...and you
          both hate me.

He turns and walks, with dignity, back into the bedroom.

                                        (CONTINUED)

                         ARMAND
              Oh, God...
                   (hurrying after him)
              Albert, we don't hate you...

Val stands alone, his face a tragic mask...and then, Agador,
dressed in a dark suit but barefoot, comes in from the
kitchen and begins setting the table.

                         AGADOR
                   (singing)
              "She works hard for the money,
              She works hard for it, honey..."

                         VAL
                   (on the edge of tears)
              You'd better put your shoes on.
              It's getting late.

                         AGADOR
                   (speaking in a strange,
                    deep voice)
              There's no point in my putting
              shoes on. I never wear shoes.
              They make me fall.

                         VAL
              Go put your shoes on, Agador. And
              talk in your normal voice. And
              just...give me a break. Please.

                         AGADOR
                   (studies him a moment)
              All right.

He bustles out. The phone begins RINGING. Val sits
listening to it, absently...then, suddenly, looks at it with
real hope.

                         VAL
              Maybe they're dead!
                   (looks at the crucifix,
                    in horror)
              You know I didn't mean that.
              What's happening to me...

The ANSWER PHONE CLICKS ON and KATHARINE'S VOICE says:

                         KATHARINE'S VOICE
              Armand? This is Katharine. I'm in
              the car and I just got a message
              telling me not to come tonight, and
              I wanted to check...

                         VAL
                   (snatching up the phone)
              It's a mistake. He said not to
              come late. I was there.

80   INT./EXT. HIGHWAY - A BMW - DRIVING - DUSK   80

Katharine steers through traffic as she speaks.   <u>CROSSCUT</u>.

                    KATHARINE
          Oh, I'm <u>so</u> glad. I <u>thought</u> my
          secretary got it wrong. I should
          be there in half an hour. Is
          this...Val?

                    VAL
               (suddenly tongue-tied)
          Yes.

                    KATHARINE
          Val...I want you to know how...how
          happy I am that I can do this for
          you. I know it's a little late...

81   ARMAND'S APARTMENT   81

                    VAL
          No. It's fine. Thank you...for
          this. See you in half an hour.
               (he hangs up)
          Mom.

                    ARMAND
          What?

Val turns. Armand has come into the room. Val quickly turns
the phone ringer off.

                    VAL
          What?

                    ARMAND
          What did you say? "See you in half
          an hour...mom"? Was that...

                    VAL
          Yes. And there's no way to call
          her back. She's in the car.

                    ARMAND
          Oh, Christ! Are you crazy? Albert
          is totally hysterical <u>now</u>. Do
          you know what he'll do if Katharine
          walks into this house...

                    VAL
          Nothing. He won't embarrass me.
          Pop, I couldn't tell her not to
          come. She's my mother. And she'll
          make the evening work. I mean,
          without her...I'm screwed. And you
          know it.

                                        (CONTINUED)

81   CONTINUED: 81

                              ARMAND
                    (he looks at the
                    crucifix)
                 So this is hell. And there's a
                 crucifix in it.

82   INT. KEELEYS' LINCOLN - DUSK   82

      The Chauffeur is driving. The Keeleys peer out the window at
      the gaudy strip, the sign that says <u>NO CRUISING WHEN YELLOW</u>
      <u>LIGHT IS FLASHING</u>...

                              MRS. KEELEY
                 This is less like Palm Beach than I
                 imagined.

                              BARBARA
                 It was...all sand when they bought
                 here. This...just...grew up around
                 them while they were in Greece.

83   INT. ARMAND'S APARTMENT - VAL, ARMAND   83

      staring at the bedroom door. Armand tries it. It is locked.

                              ARMAND
                 If we're lucky, he won't come out
                 at all.
                    (addressing the crucifix)
                 I'm not religious. And I'm Jewish.
                 But if everything goes all right
                 tonight, I'll buy you.

      The DOORBELL rings.

                              VAL
                 Amen. And speaking of Jewish.
                 Barbara told her parents our last
                 name is Coleman.

                              ARMAND
                 What!

      The DOORBELL rings again. Agador runs in wearing shoes,
      trips and falls.

                              ARMAND
                    (to the crucifix)
                 Thanks.

      Agador opens the door. The Keeleys stand there.

                              AGADOR
                 Good evening. I'm Spartacus, the
                 Goldman's butler.

                                                        (CONTINUED)

83 CONTINUED: 83

                          ARMAND
                    (to the crucifix)
            Perfect.

                          SENATOR KEELEY
            Goldman?

                          VAL
            Coldman. Spartacus is...is...

        ARMAND   VAL   BARBARA
    ...Guatemalan.   ...New.   Val, this is my father

                          BARBARA
            and mother. This is Val Coleman.

                          SENATOR KEELEY
            Coleman? or Coldman?

                          ARMAND
            Coleman. The "d" is silent.

                          VAL
            My father--

                          ARMAND
                    (he bows to Mrs. Keeley)
            How do you do...

                          MRS. KEELEY
                    (impressed by the bow)
            My daughter Barbara...

                          ARMAND
                    (bows)
            Delighted.

                          MRS. KEELEY
            My husband.

                          ARMAND
            Extremely honored.

He thrusts his hand out from the shoulder, his wrist rigid.
Senator Keeley blinks at the Frankenstein-like gesture, then
holds out his own hand. They shake.

                          SENATOR KEELEY
            You have a forceful handshake, Mr.
            Coleman.

                          ARMAND
            Well--you have to in Greece.

There is a tiny pause.

                                        (CONTINUED)

83 CONTINUED: 2   83

                          VAL
          My mother won't be here for another
          ten or fifteen minutes. She's...
          visiting my grandparents...in Palm
          Beach...and the traffic...

                       MRS. KEELEY
          Oh, isn't that nice--to have
          contact between the generations.

                        ARMAND
          Yes. Won't you come in.

Armand leads them into the living room, walking slowly and
stiffly. They watch his tortured progress.

                          VAL
          How's your leg, dad? My father has
          an old football injury.

                     SENATOR KEELEY
          Ah! I thought I recognized a
          fellow sufferer. Where did you
          play?

      VAL   ARMAND   BARBARA
   Miami, U...   Greece...   What an interesting

                        BARBARA
          room! Oh, I love it. Oh, look
          mother. Isn't this room nice?

                       MRS. KEELEY
          Yes, very. Very pleasant vacation
          house. I like its...severity.

                          VAL
          Actually, dad uses this place more
          for...work and reflection than
          anything else. It's not so much a
          vacation house as a...a...

                        ARMAND
          ...monastery.

                          VAL
          Yes.

                       MRS. KEELEY
          Well, it's just charming. And what
          lovely old books.
                  (reading the titles)
          "Nancy Drew and the Case of the
          Burning Candle." Oh, you have the
          whole series.

                                          (CONTINUED)

83   CONTINUED: 3   83

                              VAL
          What?   Yes.   They're my mother's.

                              ARMAND
          Sit down.   Please, please.

They sit on the massively soft couch and rigid Gothic chairs.

                              ARMAND
          Shall we have some champagne to
          celebrate?

                              MRS. KEELEY
          Oh, how nice.

                              ARMAND
                    (calling)
          Agador!

                              VAL
                    (quickly)
          Spartacus!

                              ARMAND
          Agador Spartacus!
                    (to the Keeleys)
          He insists on being called by his
          full name.
                    (Agador appears in the
                     doorway)
          Bring in the champagne.

Agador limps out. Val and Armand sit smiling at the
Keeleys. They are soaked with sweat.

84   EXT. THE BIRDCAGE - NIGHT   84

The silver Escort is parked in front of the club...behind
the black Lincoln. The Chauffeur sits inside.

Radman talks to the Chauffeur through the window, then walks
over to the corner where the Photographer stands snapping
pictures.

                              HARRY RADMAN
          They went in around the corner.

The Photographer looks where Radman is pointing.

                              PHOTOGRAPHER
          That's the side entrance to this
          building. I wonder if it leads to
          the club.

                              HARRY RADMAN
                    (studying it)
          Let's check it out.

85 INT. ARMAND'S LIVING ROOM - NIGHT   85

They sit in the same position we left them.

                    MRS. KEELEY
           Such a responsibility--two houses.
           How long ago did you buy this one?

                    ARMAND
           About fifteen years ago. Of
           course, the area was mostly Jewish
           then.

                    MRS. KEELEY
           Really. Barbara was telling us it
           was mostly sand.

                    ARMAND
           Yes. Well, you know the old
           saying, where there's sand...

Agador limps in with a bottle of champagne in a bucket.
He is having great difficulty walking in his shoes.

                    ARMAND
           Ah! Here we go. Champagne for
           everyone.

                    SENATOR KEELEY
           And a Scotch if you have it.

There is a little thunk from the bedroom. The Keeleys turn.

                    MRS. KEELEY
           Is someone else home?

                    ARMAND
           Just our dog, Piranha. We lock her
           in when there's company.

There is a sudden explosion as Agador opens the champagne
bottle and the cork flies across the room. Agador and
Armand squeal. Val takes the bottle from Agador.

                    VAL
           I'll finish pouring. You take care
           of dinner.

Agador teeters out. Val pours.

                    ARMAND
           He's a brilliant chef but he still
           has a lot to learn about serving.
                (glances at his watch)
           Where could my wife be.

86   EXT. CAUSEWAY OPEN - KATHARINE'S BMW IN TRAFFIC   86

The bridge is up.

Through the windshield we see Katharine pick up her cellular phone, then take out several slips of paper...

87   INT. ARMAND'S APARTMENT - NIGHT   87

Barbara and Val are talking now, their voices shrill and forced.

                        BARBARA
        ...he was like...so weird...

                        VAL
        ...I really was. I was all, "Will
        you marry me?" and she was all,
        "Excuse me? But aren't you the guy
        who said 'no way before thirty'?"

They laugh loudly.

                        BARBARA
        Oh, it was <u>so</u> funny...

                     MRS. KEELEY
        Yes, it...it <u>does</u> sound funny...

There is another thunk from the bedroom. The Keeleys' eyes dart toward the door.

                        VAL
        Did you have a good trip, Senator?

                   SENATOR KEELEY
        Uh... What? Yes. A good trip.
        Very nice. We decided to drive
        here...to see the seasons change.
        It was a long trip...down through
        Virginia, Kentucky, Tennessee,
        Georgia...but it's just so magical
        to me to come from the North where
        it's cold, to the South where it's
        warm and see the tremendous
        differences from region to region
        in this incredible country of ours.
        My wife and I used to drive down to
        Virginia every autumn to see the
        foliage turn. Virginia has amazing
        foliage--although I think the
        foliage in Ohio is underrated.
        It's just dazzling along I-75...

There is a sudden series of clicks and Katharine's Voice comes over the answerphone. Val and Armand remain motionless, their eyes fixed expectantly on the Senator's face. After a moment of uncertainty, the Senator goes on.

(CONTINUED)

SENATOR KEELEY
...just...dazzling.
But we would drive to
Virginia just to get
away for a while, you
know, see the
wonderful farms and
the countryside.
Just beautiful. The
hills...

KATHARINE'S VOICE
Hello? Hello? It's
Katharine. Armand?
Val? Albert?
Someone? Oh, shit.
Listen, I'm stuck in
traffic, can you
start dinner without
me...

Val, who has risen and backed toward the answerphone without
ever looking away from Senator Keeley, now clicks it off.

SENATOR KEELEY
...the mountains. Talk about
"purple mountains majesty"...just
fantastic. Red leaves, purple
mountains, green fields, and the
roads...black...just cutting
through the green. All the colors,
the trees...
(there is a pause)
Pennsylvania is nice, too...

There is another pause. Then, suddenly...

ARMAND
Was that my wife? Just now? On
the phone? I think it was. I
was just so caught up... Val, was
that...mom?

VAL
Yes. She's stuck and she wants us
to start dinner without her. I
should have picked up but I didn't
want to interrupt the Senator's
story.

SENATOR KEELEY
Well, it wasn't that good...

ARMAND
It was wonderful. Well, I'd better
tell Agador Spartacus the news...

He begins to swish to his feet. Val leaps to his side.

VAL
Let me help you, dad.
(to the Keeleys)
Will you excuse us?

Val leads him out of the room, onto the

73.

87A   PATIO - NIGHT   87A

                    ARMAND
              (softly)
          I've never had so much go so wrong
          so quickly. This is like a curse.

                    VAL
          What'll we do? Should we try and
          wait for her? Oh, God, this is
          awful...

87B   LIVING ROOM   87B

Senator Keeley is speaking softly to his wife.

                    SENATOR KEELEY
          Something odd is going on.

                    MRS. KEELEY
          It's this thing with Jackson. The
          wife probably doesn't want to be in
          the same house with us...and the
          father's a nervous wreck...

                    BARBARA
          Oh, no. I'm sure that's not it.

                    SENATOR KEELEY
          But there's something else...
          something about the father...and
          the butler...I can't put my finger
          on it...

                    BARBARA
          It's nothing! Why must you
          always think the worst. Val's
          mother is just a little late...

                    ARMAND
          Excuse me...

Val and Armand have returned. Val looks ashen. Armand looks
glazed.

                    ARMAND
          Well, we'll...let's give her half
          an hour and then if she isn't...

                    ALBERT'S VOICE
          Here I am!

They turn. Albert stands there, wearing a wig that has been
trimmed and sprayed into submission. There is a little stole
around his shoulders and he is carrying a purse. Armand and
Val watch, frozen.

                                              (CONTINUED)

                              ALBERT
              Please forgive me for being so late
              but the traffic was unbelievable.
              Senator Keeley, Mrs. Keeley--I'm so
              happy to meet you at last.
                    (he turns to the
                     open-mouthed Barbara)
              And you must be Barbara. What a
              pretty child! Come here and give
              me a hug. Don't be afraid. Oh,
              how adorable. She's shy.

                           MRS. KEELEY
              It's so nice to meet you, Mrs.
              Coleman.

                              ALBERT
              Goldman.

                           SENATOR KEELEY
              I thought the "d" was silent.

                           BARBARA
                    (pleadingly)
              It is pronounced Coleman, isn't
              it? We've had some confusion...

                              ALBERT
              Oh, yes. Coleman. The d is silent
              in America. It's Cole'd'Isle au
              Man or Cole of the Isle of Man in
              France where Armand's chateau is,
              and Cole d'man in Greece where
              Armand's work is, and, finally, the
              vulgar Coleman in Florida where
              Armand's home is...so, actually, we
              don't know where we are until we
              hear our last name pronounced.
                    (he laughs, trillingly)

                           MRS. KEELEY
              Oh, I see. Well, that explains
              it.

                           SENATOR KEELEY
              Yes. At last.

                           BARBARA
              I think I would like to hug you,
              Mrs. Coleman.

88   INT. A SMALL LOCAL NEWSROOM - IN NEW ENGLAND - NIGHT   88

     CAMERA tracks with a man (THE TV REPORTER) as he walks across
     the floor and into a small

89   TAPE EDIT ROOM   89

    where a PRODUCER and a TAPE EDITOR are going over the footage
    of Senator Keeley that was shot the night before.

    The Producer looks up as The Reporter enters.

                         PRODUCER
              Take a look. We were going through
              footage for the special on
              Jackson...
                   (to the editor)
              Can you pump up the sound?

90   ON SCREEN   90

    The Chauffeur reaches through the gate and takes some bills
    from Radman. There is a hiss and crackle as the images
    speak:

                         HARRY RADMAN - TAPE
              "Where are you driving him?"

                         CHAUFFEUR - ON TAPE
              "South Beach, Florida."

91   RETURN TO TAPE EDIT ROOM   91

    The Editor hits a switch. The frame freezes.

                         TV REPORTER
              Where'd we get this?

                         PRODUCER
              Keeley's house last night.
              Shooting cutaways. The fat guy is
              with The Inquirer. Harry...Radman.

                         TV REPORTER
                   (peering at the screen)
              Oh, yeah. My God, he put on so
              much weight since the Simpson case.
                   (there is a brief pause)
              Maybe this should go to the
              network.

92   INT. ARMAND'S LIVING ROOM - NIGHT   92

    They are all chatting, much more relaxed now...except for Val
    and Armand.

                         MRS. KEELEY
              It's just wonderful what you've
              done here...everything so simple
              and uncluttered.
                   (MORE)

                                                      (CONTINUED)

92   CONTINUED: 92

                              MRS. KEELEY (cont'd)
                    Our place is just a sea of
                    papers...
                              (shaking her finger at
                              Senator Keeley, jokingly)
                    You men! You're just the biggest
                    babies. They can run the world but
                    they can't pick a tie.

                              ALBERT
                    I know. I can't get this big lug
                    to buy a new suit.

                              SENATOR KEELEY
                    Armand, they're picking on us.

                              ARMAND
                         (who is outraged)
                    Yes.

                              ALBERT
                    Well, bless them, that's the way
                    nature made them. Maybe I'm just
                    an old-fashioned girl, but I pity
                    the woman who's too busy to stay
                    home and take care of her man.

          Barbara stiffens. Senator Keeley raises his glass.

                              SENATOR KEELEY
                    Hear, hear! God, it's _so_ nice to
                    meet people like you.

93   EXT. SIDE ENTRANCE - ARMAND'S BUILDING   93

          Radman is peering at the card above the bell and speaking
          into a cellular phone.

                              HARRY RADMAN
                    C-o-l-e-m-a-n. ...No first name on
                    the bell. ...You're sure?
                         (to photographer)
                    They can't find him.

                              PHOTOGRAPHER
                    What about the name on the club?
                    Goldman. Coleman and Goldman are
                    pretty damned close.

                              HARRY RADMAN
                    You're right. Wouldn't _that_ be
                    something.
                         (into phone)
                    Try Goldman. Armand Goldman.

94   INT. ARMAND'S LIVING ROOM   94

Barbara, Val, and Armand are rigid. Only the Keeleys and
Albert are at ease.

                    SENATOR KEELEY
          ...just so odd to me, this fuss
          over school prayer. As if anyone--
          Jews, Muslims, whatever, would mind
          if their children prayed in the
          classroom.

                    ALBERT
          It's insane.

Agador walks in with a bucket of ice, sees Albert and
collapses into hysterical laughter.

                    ARMAND
          Thank you, Agador Spartacus. You
          may go.

Agador puts the ice bucket down and exits.

                    ALBERT
          He's very nice but he's such a
          problem! We never know what makes
          him laugh.

                    MRS. KEELEY
          At least he speaks English. If you
          knew how many chauffeurs we've run
          through in the last six months...

                    ALBERT
          If you knew how many maids we've
          run through in the last six years.
          I could name a dozen: Rodney,
          Julian, Bruce -

                    ARMAND
          Oh, look!
               (they turn)
          You all need more ice in your
          drinks!

He picks up the ice bucket and tongs, and makes his way
around the room, dropping ice in their glasses.

                    SENATOR KEELEY
          You know, I really have such a good
          feeling about you people. Not a
          lot of "clever" books on the
          shelves, not a lot of fancy "art"
          on the walls--just the crucifix and
          a lot of good, warm, family
          feeling.
                    (MORE)

(CONTINUED)

                    SENATOR KEELEY (cont'd)
This is what Clinton didn't
understand when he started in on
school prayer and gays in the
military...

                    ARMAND
And more ice for you...

                    ALBERT
Oh, now there's an idiotic
issue--gays in the military! I
mean, those haircuts, those
uniforms--who cares?

                    VAL
Now, mom...you shouldn't be talking
about things you don't know
about. Please...

                    SENATOR KEELEY
Don't patronize your mother, Val.
She's an amazingly intelligent
woman. I think homosexuality...

                    ARMAND
And a lot more ice for you...

                    VAL
I'll have some ice, dad.

                    SENATOR KEELEY
...is one of the things that's
weakening this country.

                    ALBERT
You know, that's what I thought
until I found out Alexander the
Great, was a fag. Talk about gays
in the military.

                    ARMAND
How about those Dolphins!

They stare at him. He drops the ice bucket.

                    VAL
I'll get it.

Senator Keeley suddenly puts his drink down.

                    SENATOR KEELEY
Look, I think...we've been skirting
an issue that has Mr. Coleman very
nervous...and I don't blame him.
                    (MORE)

(CONTINUED)

94 CONTINUED: 2   94

                    SENATOR KEELEY (cont'd)
                (there is a deathly hush)
            I know you've heard the terrible
            news about Senator Jackson, how he
            died...

                        ALBERT
            Oh, <u>that</u>. Yes. What an ugly
            story. Of course, we don't believe
            a word of it.

                    SENATOR KEELEY
            What...what do you mean?

                        ALBERT
            He was obviously framed. And I,
            for one, would like an autopsy.

                        VAL
            Uh...mom...

                    SENATOR KEELEY
                (gasping)
            That's just what Rush Limbaugh
            said.

                        ARMAND
                (rising)
            Excuse me.

He hurries out, and into

95 THE KITCHEN - ARMAND   95

staggers in and quickly puts his head between his knees.
Agador hands him a drink. He tosses it back.

                        ARMAND
            I've never felt such tension. It's
            like riding a psychotic horse
            toward a burning stable.

                        AGADOR
                (deep in his own crisis)
            Dinner will be late. But I just
            had so little time to shop...

                        ARMAND
            But the girl's nice...and I owe it
            to Val. Growing up the way he
            did...it can't have been easy...

                        AGADOR
            And I'm <u>really</u> sorry about
            laughing at Miss Albert. It was
            just that <u>hairdo</u>!

                                        (CONTINUED)

95   CONTINUED:

                              ARMAND
                    Fuck it. It's one night. I can
                    live through it.

He turns and walks back into

96   INT. LIVING ROOM - NIGHT   96

just in time to hear...

                              SENATOR KEELEY
                    ...of course, it's very wrong to
                    kill an abortion doctor--

Armand clutches his heart.

                              VAL
                    Dad...

                              ARMAND
                    I'm here, son.

                              SENATOR KEELEY
                    --but many pro-lifers--I don't
                    agree with them--but many
                    sincerely believe that stopping the
                    doctors will stop the abortions.

                              ALBERT
                    Well, that's ridiculous. The
                    doctors are just doing their jobs.
                    If you're going to kill someone
                    kill the mothers. That'll stop
                    'em.

There is a moment of stunned silence.

                              ARMAND
                    Dear...may I see you for a
                    moment...

                              ALBERT
                    I know what you're going to say--if
                    you kill the mother the fetus dies
                    too, but the fetus is going to be
                    aborted anyway so why not let it go
                    down with the ship.

                              ARMAND
                    I really must see you. Now.

                              ALBERT
                    Excuse me.

He rises and follows Armand out of the room. There is
complete silence.

                                                    (CONTINUED)

96   CONTINUED: 96

                              VAL
                    I assure you...my mother is just
                    following out a train of thought to
                    its logical and absurd conclusion.
                    Very much the way Jonathan Swift
                    did when he suggested the Irish
                    peasants feed their babies to the
                    rich.

                         SENATOR KEELEY
                    Well, I don't know anything about
                    Jonathan Swift. But I know one
                    thing about your mother--she's a
                    passionate woman who follows her
                    heart. And I just love her.

97   EXT. ARMAND'S BUILDING - THE SIDE ENTRANCE   97

Radman is on the phone. The Photographer is snapping
pictures.

                         HARRY RADMAN
                         (into phone)
                    So, in other words Goldman owns the
                    club, and lives above it, and
                    owns the building...and he's
                    gay.
                         (he hangs up and turns to
                          the Photographer)
                    We're in Inquirer heaven.

98   INT. A LARGE NEWSROOM - NATIONAL STATION   98

around a big open set, with a bank of telephones and a glass
window where the EXECUTIVE PRODUCER sits, talking on the
phone. A middle-aged man with glasses (EDITOR) stands next
to him, waiting patiently.

                         EXECUTIVE PRODUCER
                         (into phone; writing)
                    ..."black Lincoln...with Ohio
                    license plates." ...Got it. ...
                    Well, it's a small area. If he's
                    there, they'll spot him.
                         (he hangs up; to the
                          Editor)
                    Kevin Keeley slipped off to South
                    Beach and the National Inquirer is
                    tracking him.
                         (hands him the slip of
                          paper)
                    Call Miami and tell them to get on
                    it. This could be real news.

82.

99 INT. ARMAND'S APARTMENT   99

    Armand is at the piano playing "I Could Have Danced All
    Night." Albert is dancing with Senator Keeley and singing in
    his ear. Val is dancing with Barbara. Mrs. Keeley is
    sitting on the bench with Armand and singing.

    ANGLE - BARBARA, VAL

                        BARBARA
              I hope your mother knows I'm going
              to have a career after we're
              married.

                        VAL
              Barbara, Albert is not my mother.
              He's a drag queen.

                        BARBARA
              That's right, that's right. I just
              can't...he just sounds so much
              like a mother.

    They arrive at the last line of the song...and Agador steps
    into the doorway and finishes with them.

                        AGADOR, THE KEELEYS, ALBERT
              "...I could have danced, danced, danced
               all night!"
                        (they burst into applause)

                        MRS. KEELEY
              What a lovely voice you have,
              Agador Spartacus.

                        AGADOR
                        (glancing at Armand,
                         bitterly)
              Thank you. Dinner is served.

    Senator Keeley offers Albert his arm. Barbara and Mrs.
    Keeley follow. Val looks at Armand.

                        ARMAND
                        (softly)
              Go on in. I'm going to write a
              note to Katharine and tape it to
              the door. Go on.

    Val goes, reluctantly, into

100 ARMAND'S DINING ROOM   100

    The guests stand at the table. Through the open doorway we
    can see Armand rushing around, looking for a piece of paper
    to write on.

                                              (CONTINUED)

100   CONTINUED: 100

                         ALBERT
              ...and Mrs. Keeley there. And the
              Senator on my left. And Val over
              there... Please sit.

                         SENATOR KEELEY
                    (putting his hand on
                     Albert's)
              You are the <u>most</u> gracious
              hostess...

                         ALBERT
                    (putting his free hand
                     over Senator Keeley's)
              Thank you. Oh, I'm having such a
              wonderful time...

101   INT. LIVING ROOM - ARMAND   101

      has now found a pad and is tearing a sheet of paper off it.
      Through the open door we see and hear the others.

                         ALBERT'S VOICE
              ...This is just what I've always
              dreamed of, a big, loving family...
              gathered around the table...just
              the way it was when I was a girl...

      Armand looks up, incredulously.

                         SENATOR KEELEY'S VOICE
              Yes, that's how we grew up, too...

                         ALBERT'S VOICE
              Oh, it was a wonderful world then,
              wasn't it? Happy families and
              everyone speaking English and no
              drugs and no AIDS...

                         VAL'S VOICE
              Easy on the wine, mom.

                         MRS. KEELEY'S VOICE
              What interesting china. It looks
              like young men playing together.
              Is it Greek?

      Armand freezes.

                         ALBERT'S VOICE
              I...I...have no idea. I've never
              seen these bowls before.

                                              (CONTINUED)

101   CONTINUED: 101

                          MRS. KEELEY'S VOICE
                  Really? Barbara, get my glasses,
                  will you dear? They're in my purse
                  on the sofa.

Barbara rises and flies into the living room toward the sofa,
nearly colliding with Armand, who is racing toward the
kitchen.

102   ARMAND'S DINING ROOM   102

Mrs. Keeley is squinting at her unused soup bowl. Senator
Keeley is searching through his pockets.

                          SENATOR KEELEY
                  Where are my glasses.
                          (lifting the bowl toward
                          his face)
                  It is Greek... Greek boys,
                  actually... Naked Greek boys...

                          ALBERT
                  And girls. Don't you have any
                  girls on your bowl?

                          VAL
                  I have one.

                          ALBERT
                  So do I.   Look, Senator Keeley.
                  There. I think that's a girl.

                          SENATOR KEELEY
                  Then it's been a long time since
                  you've seen one. That's a boy. I
                  may need glasses but I can still
                  see that.

Barbara darts in holding her mother's purse.

                          BARBARA
                  I couldn't find the glasses. Maybe
                  you left them in the car.

                          SENATOR KEELEY
                  I must have mine somewhere...
                          (rummaging in his jacket)

103   INT. ARMAND'S KITCHEN - NIGHT   103

Agador is ladling soup into a large tureen. Armand
stands holding the handles. Agador drops some shrimp in.

                                          (CONTINUED)

103   CONTINUED: 103

                              ARMAND
                    Hurry! You idiot! They're sitting
                    there looking at the bowls now.
                    What kind of moron sets the table
                    without looking at the bowls! Stop
                    ladling! Just give me the pot!

104   INT. ARMAND'S DINING ROOM - NIGHT   104

Senator Keeley is now checking his pants pockets.

                          SENATOR KEELEY
                    It just drives me so damned crazy
                    - wait - here they are.
                          (takes out his glasses,
                           puts them on)
                    Now let's look and see what these
                    Greeks are doing.

He looks down at the bowl just as Armand sweeps in and ladles
the soup into it.

                              ARMAND
                    Here we go. We're in luck. Some
                    of Agador's superb soup!...

He ladles the soup into Mrs. Keeley's bowl.

                              ARMAND
                    Hmmm. And it's his specialty.
                    Seafood chowder.

                          MRS. KEELEY
                          (staring at the ladle)
                    Isn't...that a hard boiled egg?

                              ARMAND
                    What? Why...yes. It...is! This
                    is so "Guatemala." They put hard
                    boiled eggs in everything down
                    there. Well, chicken is so
                    important to them. It's their only
                    real currency. A woman is said to
                    be worth her weight in hens. A
                    man's wealth is measured by the
                    size of his cock. Do you all have
                    soup? Yes. Would you excuse me?

105   INT. KITCHEN - ARMAND   105

storms in. Agador stands clutching a dishtowel.

                              ARMAND
                    What the hell are you serving us.

                                                      (CONTINUED)

105   CONTINUED: 105

                                AGADOR
                    Sweet and sour peasant soup. I
                    don't know why you called it
                    seafood chowder.

                                ARMAND
                    What's sweet and sour peasant soup?

                                AGADOR
                    I don't know. I made it up.

                                ARMAND
                    Oh, my God! This is a nightmare.

106   INT. ARMAND'S DINING ROOM - NIGHT   106

        They are eating their soup in a new, slightly awkward
        silence. Armand is not at the table. Val keeps glancing
        toward the kitchen and at his watch.

                                ALBERT
                    Where are you staying in Florida?

                                MRS. KEELEY
                    With the Bushes on Fisher Island.
                    The Jeb Bushes.

                                ALBERT
                    Oh, Fisher Island. Such a lovely
                    spot. My parents lived on Fisher
                    Island until they died.

        Val shakes his head, violently.

                                SENATOR KEELEY
                    Weren't you just visiting your
                    parents in Palm Beach?

                                ALBERT
                    What? Yes. Now. That they're
                    dead. They've moved. Were moved.
                    Because... my mother always said
                    "live on Fisher Island, get buried
                    in Palm Beach, that way you'll have
                    the best of Florida."

                                VAL
                         (springing up)
                    Excuse me.

        He rushes into

107   THE KITCHEN - NIGHT   107

    Agador is weeping in the corner. Armand stands with his
    forehead pressed against the wall.

                        VAL
          Dad! You've got to get in there!
          Everything's going to hell...

    He breaks off as Armand turns and looks at him with insane
    eyes.

                   ARMAND
          He didn't make an entree.

                      VAL
          What do you mean? You mean...we
          just have <u>soup</u>?

                  AGADOR
            (sobbing)
          Peasant soup <u>is</u> an entree. It's
          like a stew. That's why I put so
          much in it...

                  ARMAND
          Shut up.
            (he thrusts a piece of
             paper into Val's hands)
          Here! It's the note for Katharine.
          Put it on the outside door. I have
          to get back before they eat enough
          to see the bottom of the bowl.

                  AGADOR
          I had an hour to shop, I had a
          million things to do...

                  ARMAND
          Shut <u>up</u>. All right, all right,
          stop crying, it's done. Goddamn
          you.
            (to Val)
          Why are you standing there! <u>Go</u>!
          She'll be here any minute.

                      VAL
            (suddenly coming to life)
          Oh, <u>man</u>!
            (he streaks out)

108   EXT. STREET - NIGHT - KATHARINE'S BMW   108

    as it passes the <u>NO CRUISING WHEN LIGHT IS FLASHING</u>. She
    looks at her watch, shakes her head.

109   EXT. SOUTH BEACH - NIGHT - A WHITE VAN   109

with the letters WXLT on the side moving slowly down the
street.

110   INT./EXT. WHITE VAN - NIGHT   110

A Young Editor and his pretty blond assistant (FAYE). The
Editor is driving. Faye peers out the window, a slip of
paper clutched in her hand. The Editor suddenly straightens.

                         YOUNG EDITOR
               Up ahead. See if the black Lincoln
               has Ohio plates.

                         FAYE
               Where?

                         YOUNG EDITOR
               With the chauffeur leaning against
               it.

                         FAYE
                    (squinting at it, then at
                     the paper)
               That's it. Pull over.

They pull into the only parking space on the street--in
between the silver Escort and the black Lincoln--just as
Katharine's BMW U-turns to get the same space.

The Editor sticks his head out of the window.

                         YOUNG EDITOR
                    (calling to Katharine)
               Sorry.

Katharine swears softly, U-turns again, and inches forward
looking for another parking space.

111   EXT. ARMAND'S BUILDING - SIDE ENTRANCE - NIGHT - VAL   111

taping the note to the front door. He peers down the street,
anxiously...then opens the door and darts back in.

The moment he is gone, Radman and the Cameraman step out of
the shadows. Radman grabs the note.

                         HARRY RADMAN
                    (reading)
               "Katharine--whatever you do, don't
               go upstairs. I'll call you
               tomorrow. Armand."
                    (he puts the note in his
                     pocket)
               This is going to be great.

112   INT. DINING ROOM - NIGHT   112

>   They are just finishing the soup. Val's chair is still
>   empty. The Keeleys' eyes keep darting toward it.

>   ALBERT
>   ...and from that day on, they
>   decided to look for a cemetery they
>   really loved instead of eating
>   tofu. Daddy favored Key Biscayne
>   but mummy was afraid of
>   developers...

>   ARMAND
>   Senator Keeley?

>   He leaps up with the tureen.

>   SENATOR KEELEY
>   No, no...

>   Armand ladles in another bowlful.

>   SENATOR KEELEY
>   (firmly)
>   Thank you. No more after this. I
>   don't want to get too full.

>   ARMAND
>   No fear of that. Mrs. Keeley?

>   She puts her hands over her bowl as Armand approaches.

>   MRS. KEELEY
>   No, really. I'm saving myself for
>   the main course.

>   ARMAND
>   Oh, but I thought you understood...

>   He lowers the ladle and, in a daring move, begins to tilt it.
>   Mrs. Keeley whips her hands out of the way just as the liquid
>   cascades into her bowl.

>   ARMAND
>   ...this is the main course. In
>   the Guatemalan jungle, peasant soup
>   represents a coming together or
>   pot-au-feu, everything in one
>   pot--actually, everyone in one
>   pot--as they say in Agador's little
>   village on bath night.
>   (he laughs, ignoring
>   their uneasy faces)
>   (MORE)

(CONTINUED)

                              ARMAND (cont'd)
                    But, seriously, when two families
                    are about to unite, they dine
                    together on peasant soup for the
                    first meal--to symbolize that
                    they're both going to be in the
                    same...

                              ALBERT
                    ...pot.

                              ARMAND
                    Yes.

                              BARBARA
                    Oh, that's so...incredible. Don't
                    you think that's incredible, dad?

                              SENATOR KEELEY
                    Yes.

                              BARBARA
                    And this is such a great dish.
                    Don't you think so, mom?

                              MRS. KEELEY
                    Yes. What...what gives the soup
                    greens that sweetish taste.

                              SENATOR KEELEY
                         (chewing)
                    The pineapple.

Val sprints in, breathlessly.

                              ARMAND
                    Well, just in time for dessert.
                    Did you get everything done?

                              VAL
                    Yes.

                              ALBERT
                         (rising)
                    Then shall we have our coffee in
                    the living room?

They stop in mid-mouthful...then put down their spoons and
get to their feet.

113   EXT. THE BIRDCAGE - NIGHT   113

The white van is parked behind the black Lincoln. Faye, the
blond assistant, is standing at the curb with the Keeleys'
chauffeur--handing him money. A few feet away, the Young
Editor stands talking, excitedly, on a cellular phone.

114   EXT. A STREET - NIGHT - KATHARINE'S BMW   114

The street is darker, the music distant.

Katharine finishes parking, her rear and front bumpers
touching the cars on either side. She opens the door and
nearly falls out...then looks at her watch and starts
running.

115   INT. ARMAND'S LIVING ROOM - NIGHT   115

They are seated on the couch, drinking coffee and eating the
cake that used to say "To my piglet, from his uncle."

Barbara looks haggard. Val is dazed. Armand's suit is
crumpled, his collar crushed, his tie out. Albert's lipstick
has melted. But they are still working.

                         ARMAND
               So...what do you think about these
               kids getting married?

                    SENATOR KEELEY
               Well...of course...she's only
               eighteen and he's only twenty and
               so, naturally...

There is the sudden BLAST OF MUSIC O.S., and we hear the
opening number begin downstairs.

                    SENATOR KEELEY
               Good God...that sounds like it's
               coming from downstairs.

                    MRS. KEELEY
                  (listening)
               It is. It must be from the
               nightclub on the corner.
               This...this must be the same
               building.

                         ALBERT
               You're joking! I always thought
               that was someone's television set.

                         ARMAND
                  (chuckling, quickly)
               Now, mother--you know we live
               above a nightclub.
                  (to the Keeleys)
               My wife has traveled all over the
               world with me but, deep down, she's
               still the same little girl from
               Grovers Corners.

                         ALBERT
               Yes. I'm afraid I am a bit
               naive.

                                        (CONTINUED)

                         SENATOR KEELEY
                    (leaning forward;
                     suddenly, fiercely)
               Don't you be ashamed of Grovers
               Corners, Mrs. Coleman. It may not
               be a chateau in France but it's a
               damned good place to call home.

They look at him, taken aback by his intensity. The music is
quite loud now...and there is a slight vibration from the
dancing.

                         ALBERT
               Oh, thank you, I will remember
               that. Of course, Armand is much
               more sophisticated than I am, but
               he comes from good stock...
                    (his wig slips)
               ...and so do these two
               youngsters...

Barbara sees the wig and jumps up, in front of Albert.

                         BARBARA
               Where's the bathroom?

                         VAL
                    (standing up)
               I'll show you.

                         BARBARA
               No. I want...Mother Coleman to
               show me.

                         ALBERT
                    (rising; his hand to his
                     heart)
               Oh, my dear child...
                    (tears fill his eyes)

Armand suddenly sees Albert's crooked wig, leaps up, and
grasps Albert's head in his hands, trying to straighten it.

                         ARMAND
               One kiss.

                         ALBERT
                    (pushing him away)
               Armand, I'm only going to the
               bathroom.

The wig is now slightly worse. Val moves to the other side
of Albert.

                                                    (CONTINUED)

                          VAL
            We'll all go. That's a pretty
            tough door to handle since the
            paint job.

                          ALBERT
            Well, I think you're all crazy.
                 (shakes his head, the wig
                  wobbles)
            My men.

Albert starts toward the bathroom, with Armand and Val
crowded in on either side of him, their arms around his
waist. Barbara leans her cheek against Albert's as they
walk, covering him from the front.

                          BARBARA
            This is so wonderful...all of us
            together, all of us pot-au-feu.

                          ALBERT
            Oh, I think I'm going to cry. Oh,
            my goodness...I'm so happy.

He begins to weep as they walk him out of the room. The
Keeleys sit staring after them.

                          MRS. KEELEY
            Something very strange is going
            on here.

                          SENATOR KEELEY
            I know.

                          MRS. KEELEY
            That dinner. And I know there
            was something on those bowls. And
            the son disappearing like that
            while we were eating...

                          SENATOR KEELEY
            I know just what's going on.

                          MRS. KEELEY
            You do?

                          SENATOR KEELEY
            Of course, I do. It's the oldest
            story in the world.

                          MRS. KEELEY
            What is it?

                                        (CONTINUED)

                    SENATOR KEELEY
          She's a small-town girl and he's a
          pretentious European--the worst
          kind--with his Cole d' whatever and
          his decadent china. Oh, I've seen
          this before. Aristotle Onassis
          was like this, and all the
          French, especially Mitterand, and
          the English--not Margaret Thatcher,
          of course, but you can't tell me
          John Major doesn't have something
          on the side, and she just can't
          handle it.

                    MRS. KEELEY
          Who?

                    SENATOR KEELEY
          Mrs. Coleman.

                    MRS. KEELEY
          Why should she care about John
          Major.

                    SENATOR KEELEY
          No, no. Mrs. Coleman can't
          handle her marriage, to him, to
          Coleman, with his nasty little
          European traditions, and his
          snobbery, and that dig about
          Grovers Corners...

                    MRS. KEELEY
          Kevin, you're rambling.

                    SENATOR KEELEY
          Well, it makes me furious to see
          the contempt he has for her. Did
          you see him while she was talking?
          He looked...almost frightened. And
          the son is patronizing, too. And
          that fake European courtliness --
          "one kiss," and the way he bowed
          when he was introduced to you. And
          he doesn't even let her run the
          house. He's in the kitchen,
          and he serves, and he tells
          that beige savage what to do...

116 INT. BEDROOM - ALBERT, ARMAND, BARBARA, VAL   116

Albert is weeping in earnest now, his wig askew. Masses of
hair strewn around the dressing table indicate what the wig
once was. Armand, Val, and Barbara search through drawers
and shelves.

                                        (CONTINUED)

                        ALBERT
          I'm sorry. I'm so sorry. I've
          ruined everything.

                        ARMAND
          Don't be silly. No one even
          noticed the wig. Where the hell is
          the spirit gum.

                        VAL
          I don't know. They carted
          everything out of here...

                        BARBARA
          I have a barrette. Let's try it.
          If you don't move your head too
          much, it might work...

                        ALBERT
          Thank you, you're a very sweet
          girl. Oh, Val, I'm so sorry...

117   INT. LIVING ROOM - NIGHT   117

The Keeleys are standing now, their faces tight with anger.

                        MRS. KEELEY
          Well, I notice you didn't have this
          kind of blind sympathy for poor
          Bessie Jackson!

                        SENATOR KEELEY
          Bessie Jackson is an insensitive
          cow. This woman is a lady. For
          God's sake, I don't understand you.
          She's going to be your in-law, too.

                        MRS. KEELEY
          Well, if you think he's so terrible
          maybe Barbara shouldn't marry his
          son.

                        SENATOR KEELEY
          I don't think he's terrible in that
          way. I mean, he's not going to get
          mixed up in some stupid scandal.
          Europeans are like Republicans--
          they don't sleep with women who go
          on "A Current Affair." Except for
          that moron Jackson.

                        MRS. KEELEY
                    (staring at him)
          I don't think I've ever seen you
          before.

                                          (CONTINUED)

                       SENATOR KEELEY
         What do you mean?

                       MRS. KEELEY
         I don't even know who you are. You
         aren't even worried about Barbara.
         Just your career. And "poor little
         Mrs. Coleman."

                       SENATOR KEELEY
         Oh, please. You're just as worried
         about my career as I am. _You're_
         the one who pushed for this
         marriage. And Barbara can handle
         that boy. She's a modern woman--
         tough as nails. But Mrs. Coleman
         cries if you call her "Mother."
         She's that vulnerable. My God, it
         just breaks my heart. They don't
         make women like that anymore.

There is a knock on the door. A breathless voice calls:

                     KATHARINE'S VOICE
         Hello? I'm home. I forgot my key.

                       SENATOR KEELEY
         Who...who is it?

                     KATHARINE'S VOICE
         It's Val's mother. Mrs. Goldman.
         Is Armand there?

There is a pause.

                       SENATOR KEELEY
         Val's _mother_?

                       MRS. KEELEY
         Mrs. _Goldman_?

                     KATHARINE'S VOICE
         Hello? Armand? Open up!

                       SENATOR KEELEY
         So _this_ is the _whole_ story.
         This son-of-a-bitch has a live-in
         mistress.

Agador stumbles in, hurriedly.

           AGADOR   MRS. KEELEY
        (calling)   (calling)
    You're in the wrong   Coming!
    house.

                                   (CONTINUED)

Agador and Mrs. Keeley both race toward the door. Mrs.
Keeley wins easily. She opens it. Katharine stands there.
Agador leaps forward.

                    AGADOR
          Good evening. May I take your
          purse...as usual. Or...for the
          first time.

                    KATHARINE
          Thank you.

She hands it to him...and turns to the Keeleys.

                    KATHARINE
          You must be...Senator and Mrs.
          Keeley. Katharine Goldman. I'm
          delighted to meet you. Please
          forgive me for being so terribly
          late, but I...

She breaks off as Albert's voice rings out...

                    ALBERT'S VOICE
          Sorry to take so long but Barbara
          wanted to see the...

They turn as Albert sweeps in from the bedroom, wig secured,
followed by Val, Armand, and Barbara. They stop as they see
Katharine.

                    ALBERT
               (pointing)
          What is she doing here!

                    ARMAND
          Let me explain...

                    SENATOR KEELEY
          Yes! Explain to all of us!
               (he nods toward Albert)
          I don't want to embarrass this
          lovely lady... But exactly how many
          mothers does your son have?

                    ARMAND
          What?

                    SENATOR KEELEY
               (indicating Katharine)
          This woman has just introduced
          herself as Val's mother. How many
          mothers does Val have?

There is a pause...and then Val steps forward.

                                          (CONTINUED)

117   CONTINUED: 3   117

                                VAL
                   Just one.

He walks over to Albert and takes off the wig.

                                VAL
                   This is my mother.

Senator Keeley stands staring at Albert, blankly. Mrs.
Keeley shrinks back. Albert bursts into tears. Val puts his
arm around him.

                                VAL
                   My father owns the nightclub
                   downstairs. My mother is the star.
                   Agador's real name is Jake, he's
                   from New Jersey.

                          SENATOR KEELEY
                       (his eyes dimming)
                   What...

                                VAL
                   We lied to you. Barbara and I...
                   and everybody lied for us. These
                   are my parents.

                             ARMAND
                       (taking Albert's hand)
                   And this is my wife.
                       (he turns to Katharine)
                   And this is the lady who had Val.

                                VAL
                   Nice to meet you, Katharine.

                            KATHARINE
                   Very nice, Val.
                       (to Armand)
                   You've done a good job.

                             ARMAND
                   Thank you...
                       (he puts his hand on
                        Albert's shoulder)
                   We're very proud of him.

                          SENATOR KEELEY
                   I don't understand.

                           MRS. KEELEY
                   Wait a minute...the nightclub
                   downstairs...he owns it?
                       (she turns to Barbara)
                   You mean, he's not a cultural
                   attache...?

                                              (CONTINUED)

                              BARBARA
          No. And he's not married to a
          housewife. And their name isn't
          Coleman. It's Goldman. They're
          Jewish.

                          SENATOR KEELEY
          I don't understand.

                            MRS. KEELEY
          He's a man. They're both men.

                          SENATOR KEELEY
          He can't be.
               (to Albert)
          You can't be Jewish.

                            MRS. KEELEY
          Kevin! This is a <u>man</u>!

                          SENATOR KEELEY
               (blinking)
          What?

                              BARBARA
          Don't you understand? They're gay.
          They own the drag club downstairs.
          They're two men!

                              ALBERT
               (stepping forward)
          I just want you to know, Senator
          Keeley, that I meant every word I
          said to you about a return to
          family values and a stricter moral
          code.

                          SENATOR KEELEY
          I feel like I'm insane.

                             KATHARINE
          Look, it's very simple. Armand and
          I were together one night...

                          SENATOR KEELEY
               (to Albert)
          You <u>cried</u>. You said...you...I
          don't...

                              ALBERT
          Kevin, nothing's changed. It's
          still me. With one tiny
          difference.

                          SENATOR KEELEY
               (whispering)
          I don't understand...

                                              (CONTINUED)

>   MRS. KEELEY
>   I'll explain it to you in the car.
>   Let's go. Barbara...

>   BARBARA
>   No. I'm not coming.

>   MRS. KEELEY
>   Don't do this to me, Barbara. I
>   may not be as "vulnerable" as Mrs.
>   Coleman...but I still have
>   feelings...
>   (she breaks down)
>   ...someone has to like me best.

They stare at her. She sobs, wildly. Senator Keeley shakes
his head, as if waking from a dream...then goes over to her.

>   SENATOR KEELEY
>   Take it easy. Take it easy,
>   Louise.
>   (he looks around, looks
>   at Albert, looks away)
>   Barbara...we're leaving. And I
>   want you to come with us.

>   BARBARA
>   Daddy, please...

>   SENATOR KEELEY
>   Barbara, I've made your mother cry,
>   I'm coming up for re-election,
>   we're in the middle of a scandal,
>   and I'm in the home of a gay couple
>   who own a drag club. Now, I
>   understand that you want to get
>   married, but how many lives do you
>   want to ruin to do it.

Barbara looks at her father and her weeping mother...then,
helplessly, at Val and Armand and Albert.

>   BARBARA
>   (barely able to speak)
>   I would have...I would have...
>   really liked to have you as my
>   family.

She goes quickly to her father. He opens the door, then
turns to Albert.

>   SENATOR KEELEY
>   I just want to say, Mr...Mrs...
>   Mr...whatever your name is, that I
>   hope this won't influence your
>   vote.

(CONTINUED)

117   CONTINUED: 6   117

                              HARRY RADMAN (V.O.)
                    Senator Keeley!

Senator Keeley jumps, startled, and his hand shoots up in
front of his face. A flashbulb goes off.

He leaps back in and slams the door.

                              SENATOR KEELEY
                    Oh, <u>no</u>!

118   INT. ARMAND'S HALLWAY - NIGHT   118

Radman and the Photographer stand near the top of the stairs.

                              HARRY RADMAN
                    Did you get him?

                              PHOTOGRAPHER
                    No! I would have if you hadn't
                    said "Senator Keeley."

                              HARRY RADMAN
                    I was trying to make him turn.

119   EXT. STREET OUTSIDE THE BIRDCAGE - NIGHT   119

There is a WXLT VAN parked outside and a cameraman setting up
lights.

ANOTHER VAN with the letters WLLS draws up to the corner. A
Crewman jumps out and calls to the blond assistant, Faye.

                              CREWMAN
                    What's the story?

                              FAYE
                    If you don't know, what are you
                    doing here?

                              CREWMAN
                    We got a call that <u>you</u> were here.

120   EXT. 2ND ENTRANCE - NIGHT   120

As Radman and the Photographer come out of the door...and
stand staring bitterly at the corner.

                              HARRY RADMAN
                    Those vultures.

121   INT. ARMAND'S LIVING ROOM - NIGHT   121

Senator Keeley lies stretched out on the chaise. Mrs. Keeley
applies ice to the back of his neck. Barbara stands weeping
in the corner in Val's arms. Armand sits brooding in a
chair. Agador passes a bottle around.

Katharine sits eating a bowl of soup. Albert is at the
window.

                    ALBERT
          Another television van just
          arrived. And a car. It says
          Florida Eagle--oh, that's just
          print news.

                    SENATOR KEELEY
          They have a great headline.
          "Senator Jackson and his women:
          Senator Keeley and his men."

                    MRS. KEELEY
          But it's perfectly innocent. You
          just came to meet the parents of
          the boy Barbara wants to marry.
          And you didn't know...

                    SENATOR KEELEY
          Louise, the people of this country
          aren't interested in details. They
          don't even <u>trust</u> details. They
          just trust headlines.

                    KATHARINE
          Well, if I can put in my two cents:
          they don't have a thing on you.
          It's their word against yours that
          you're even here.

                    SENATOR KEELEY
          Well, they <u>will</u> have something on
          me. Because at some point I'll
          have to leave. People will notice
          if I'm never seen again.
               (to his wife)
          More candy.

There is a short, brooding pause.

                    ALBERT
               (looking out the window)
          Another TV crew. And they're going
          into the club. Wouldn't you know
          it. The one night I don't
          perform...

                    AGADOR
          Can I get anyone some soup?

                                        (CONTINUED)

121 CONTINUED: 121

There is a quick murmur of "no's." Katharine looks up from
her bowl.

                    KATHARINE
          Who <u>made</u> this?

                    AGADOR
          I did.

                    KATHARINE
          And it's wonderful.

                    BARBARA
          Daddy, I'm sorry...

                    SENATOR KEELEY
               (wearily)
          I know, I know...

                    AGADOR
          Another shot, Senator?

                    SENATOR KEELEY
          I don't really drink.

                    AGADOR
          Now is the time to pretend.

Armand clicks the monitor on. We hear Cyril's voice:

                    CYRIL'S VOICE
          And now we end as we began--our
          first number is our last number...

                    VOICES
               (singing)
          "We are family,
           I got all my sisters and me..."

                    VAL
          Dad, couldn't the Keeleys slip out
          with the audience at the end of the
          show?

                    ARMAND
          No. They're waiting for that.
          They'd be recognized in two
          seconds.

                    ALBERT
          Not necessarily.

122 OMITTED   122

123   INT. THE BIRDCAGE - BACKSTAGE - ARMAND   123

talking into the mike.

                    ARMAND
            A big hand for our girls, ladies
            and gentlemen!

ANGLE - THE HOUSE

The girls are trouping onstage--two by two. Armand's voice
continues over the shot.

                    ARMAND'S VOICE
            As we come to the end of our show,
            you are family, too. Please sing
            along.

There is applause. Scattered through the audience are
Newsmen, Reporters, and a few Photographers, their eyes
darting around the darkened club, searching for their prey.

Suddenly, several of the Newsmen stiffen as Armand comes from
backstage and begins making his way through the club.

                    YOUNG EDITOR
        Who's that?

                    FAYE
            Well, it's not Kevin Keeley.

Their eyes follow him as he pauses to speak to the drag
queen at the cash register (ZA-ZA) and two other drag
queens who work in the house.

ANGLE - ARMAND, ZA-ZA, TWO OTHER DRAG QUEENS

as they head briskly back toward the stage...and disappear
through the door.

124   EXT. THE BIRDCAGE - NIGHT   124

Another truck pulls up. The media is now divided between
the inside of the club, the outside of the club, and the
side entrance.

Senator Keeley's Chauffeur stands by the Lincoln, taking
money from a man in a windbreaker. There is a small line of
newsmen behind him, each holding a wad of bills.

125   EXT. SIDE STREET ENTRANCE - NIGHT   125

Radman from The Inquirer and his Photographer are squeezed
near the front of a small horde of newsmen.

                                            (CONTINUED)

125   CONTINUED: 125

                              PHOTOGRAPHER
                    How long do you think these guys
                    will wait?

                              HARRY RADMAN
                    As long as it takes. There's no
                    story if they don't get him coming
                    out.

126   INT. THE BIRDCAGE - NIGHT   126

      IN THE HOUSE the newsmen glance at their watches, shifting
      impatiently as...

      ONSTAGE Armand, Za-Za, the other two drag queens, Cyril and
      Albert stream in from the wings and join the girls as they
      begin dancing down the stairs into the house. There are
      excited cries from the crowd.

127
THRU   OMITTED   127
131   THRU
                                                                    131

132   ANGLE - TWO NEWSMEN   132

      Watching the girls mingle with the audience.

                              NEWSMAN #1
                    Oh, great.

                              NEWSMAN #2
                    I hate shows that do this.

133   OMITTED   133

134   ANGLE - SENATOR KEELEY - IN THE HOUSE   134

      sashaying around the tables, mouthing indistinguishable
      lyrics off beat, pretending to sing.

                              SENATOR KEELEY
                    "And we da-dum thing
                    birds dee feather..."

135   ANGLE - ARMAND   135

      He stops beside Val and says, softly:

                              ARMAND
                    Keep 'em moving toward the door.

136   ANGLE - MRS. KEELEY, A CUSTOMER - DANCING   136

He is an extremely handsome Latino.

                    LATINO MAN
                 (he dips her)
            I've never danced with a man
            before.

                    MRS. KEELEY
                 (throatily)
            There's always a first time.

137   ANGLE - SENATOR KEELEY, BARBARA   137

They are the only ones no one has asked to dance.

                    SENATOR KEELEY
            No one will dance with me in this
            dress. I told them white would
            make me look fat.

                    BARBARA
            I don't understand. I'm as pretty
            as the rest of these guys.

Suddenly Val comes up to them.

                    VAL
            Dance?

Both Senator Keeley and Barbara crowd into his arms.

                    VAL
            Not you, Barbara.

                    SENATOR KEELEY
                 (clutching him)
            No, don't leave me. I don't want
            to be the only girl not dancing.

                    VAL
            Just keep moving toward the door.
            We'll be out of here in a minute.

He dances away. Senator Keeley looks around, nervously,
tense and embarrassed. A tuxedoed Albert suddenly steps up
to him.

                    ALBERT
            Care to dance...
                 (his voice drops)
            ...baby.

The Senator steps gratefully into his arms, and they and the
rest of the girls continue to dance and sing their way to the
club entrance and right on out the door, waving to the crowd
as they go.

138   EXT. CLUB ENTRANCE - NEWSPEOPLE   138

turn as the SOUND of the music suddenly grows louder, the
club doors open and the girls plus Keeleys twirl out, still
dancing with customers and each other, still singing and
waving as they dance across the street...and then, disperse
in all directions.

139   EXT. ACROSS THE STREET FROM THE CLUB - NIGHT   139

Katharine sits in her car, double-parked, the motor idling,
the back door open...as the Senator, Mrs. Keeley, and Barbara
dance toward her with the others.

140   ANGLE - SENATOR KEELEY   140

As he dances past his chauffeur and whispers to him...

                    SENATOR KEELEY
              Meet me in twenty minutes on the
              corner of El Dorado and Palm...

                    CHAUFFEUR
              Lady, not for a million dollars.

Mrs. Keeley shoves the Senator into the car, the door
slams...and the car drives off into the night.

THE MOVIE CONTINUES UNDER THE FINAL CREDITS:

141   INT. A NEW ENGLAND CHURCH   141

A wedding is about to begin.

On the RIGHT SIDE OF THE CHURCH, Mrs. Keeley sits with
friends and relatives--all wealthy, tastefully groomed,
traditionally dressed...and barely able to keep their eyes
off...

THE LEFT SIDE OF THE CHURCH--where Albert and Armand sit
with their friends and relatives: Katharine, the Goldman
girls, Tony and his wife, the Greengrocer and the Butcher
and their wives, Albert's mother and two brothers, Armand's
aunt and uncle, etc.

There are FOUR USHERS, one of them Chuck, one of them a
college friend of Val's we have never seen before, and
Agador, who now limps down the aisle seating latecomers.

THE BRIDESMAIDS are lovely, gentile girls. THE MATRON OF
HONOR looks like Queen Elizabeth and stares, helplessly,
at Agador.

A priest and a rabbi are in attendance. The rabbi is gay.

142   ANGLE - THE LEFT SIDE - ZA-ZA AND A 2ND DRAG QUEEN   142

staring openly at the right side.

> ZA-ZA
> Robert Dole is <u>gorgeous</u>.

143   ANGLE - THE RIGHT SIDE   143

At the end of the row we see Robert Dole, staring fixedly
ahead. TWO MATRONS glance covertly at the left side.

> MATRON #1
> Which one is the mother?

> MATRON #2
> I just don't know.

The music begins playing and Barbara walks down the aisle
on Senator Keeley's arm.

The guests on the right side of the church watch with
softened faces. Mrs. Keeley weeps, quietly.

The guests on the left side of the church clutch their
hearts. Armand and Albert sob.

The bride reaches the altar and looks at the groom. The
groom smiles at her...and the ceremony begins.

THE END

STILLS & VOICES

I can't imagine anyone else in any of these parts. It's the only time in my life that I haven't thought, "Well, this one character, I should have gotten so-and-so." It was exactly the actors who should have been these characters. Every single one, right down to the nonspeaking parts.

—Mike Nichols

ARMAND GOLDMAN
Robin Williams

ALBERT
Nathan Lane

LOUISE KEELEY
Dianne Wiest

SENATOR KEELEY
Gene Hackman

AGADOR
Hank Azaria

KATHARINE
Christine Baranski

VAL GOLDMAN
Dan Futterman

BARBARA KEELEY
Calista Flockhart

The movie loves them all; the story doesn't take sides, you love all of them.
—Mike Nichols

THE REASON I CHOSE THIS CHARACTER is because it's a dry, restrained comedy versus being so outrageous. And that's what was interesting for me. It's like learning a whole set of different muscles.

—Robin Williams

What I wanted from Robin was this sort of suppressed hysteria, somebody who can be perfectly ordinary, with just a little something under the surface that he can't completely control. And he did it completely brilliantly, the occasional uncontrolled scream out of this perfectly manly guy.

—Mike Nichols

MIKE NICHOLS: I FIRST SAW NATHAN in a Neil Simon play, *Laughter on the 23rd Floor,* in which he played Sid Caesar. And Nathan was astonishing.

NATHAN LANE: Mike came backstage afterward and was very, very gracious and sweet and said, "I'd like to talk to you about a movie, *La Cage aux Folles.*" He said, "We've just gotten the rights, and I want Robin Williams to play the other character and Elaine May is going to write the script, what do you think?" I said, "Well, that's not too shabby." I was bouncing off the walls. I've been doing this acting thing about twenty years now. And so to have someone like Mike Nichols walk in and say, "I'd like you to star in a movie," it was like a dream.

MIKE NICHOLS: And then, for a while, Nathan couldn't do it because he had another show he was contracted to do. He called me and said he was very sorry, but he had been talking to his agents and his lawyers and it just wasn't going to be possible for him to do the movie. And I thought, "He's so calm!" It turned out he wasn't calm at all, he just had been told that there was nothing he could do. And then we worked it out. The producer of the play was a friend of mine, and he redid the schedule; and we changed ours, and it became possible.

ALBERT AND ARMAND ARE A COUPLE, and they have the same dynamics as any couple, straight or gay. They have the same problems, they're trying to get through life and deal with each other's insecurities and habits. And that's what makes it interesting.

—Robin Williams

Robin and I sort of had an instant chemistry and rapport. He started to improvise, I joined in with him, and I think he felt, "Oh, well, it's a kindred spirit."

—Nathan Lane

Working with Nathan is good because we do have this kind of great rapport. So it's like a great comedy team.

—Robin Williams

It was certainly one of the two happiest times I've ever had on a picture, the other one being *Carnal Knowledge*. It was just a group of people with no wrong ones and everybody loving everyone else and having a good time. And at the heart of it was Robin's central act of handing the torch to Nathan, as it were, and saying, "Go for it, just do anything you think of, do what you want. I'm there with you, I'm your partner."

—Mike Nichols

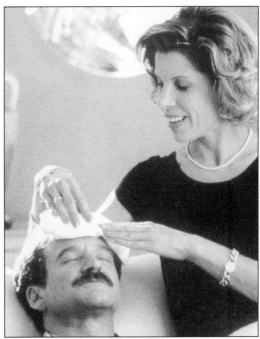

I'VE KNOWN GENE FOR A LONG TIME and knew that he started out, as I did, in improvisational comedy. I know how funny he can be, 100 percent true and funny at the same time.

—Mike Nichols

There's been a lot of laughing on this movie, falling-down laughing: Gene Hackman in tears, Dianne Wiest, everyone.

—Nathan Lane

DIANNE IS NOT ONLY A MARVELOUS ACTRESS BUT ALSO A BRILLIANT COMEDIENNE. And just as there was a remarkable generosity on the set between Robin and Nathan, the same was true with Gene and Dianne. Dianne told me it was the sweetest experience of her working life.

—Mike Nichols

We were all guilty of ruining takes. We went in the morning and we laughed until we wrapped at night. Mike would have to leave our set and go to another far away with his monitor, so that he didn't ruin the take with his laughter.

—Dianne Wiest

I WAS VERY LUCKY IN CHOOSING BO WELSH AS ART DIRECTOR AND ANN ROTH AS COSTUME DESIGNER. It was Bo who led us to South Beach and Bo who created this wonderful sort of hot Florida look. He's a great art director and Ann Roth is a great costume designer. She knows what everybody should wear, even when it's just a T-shirt and shorts. She has such a great sense of character.

Their ability to make a metaphor out of the truth, out of the accurate observation of what these particular characters would wear, how they would live, where they would live—this is of immeasurable importance. They were part of our great happiness on this movie because we were endlessly excited by the sets and the clothes when we saw them. In the beginning, getting ready, working with them both, I was as happy as I've ever been because they loved the challenge and they brought so much to it.

—Mike Nichols

The apartment set goes from Mediterranean Greek Deco all the way to *Field and Stream,* and then they pull it back to early Vatican.

—Robin Williams

THE DANCERS CAST IN THE DRAG ROLES came in to test the makeup for the first time, and they wanted to do it, they wanted it to work, but they could not believe that it would work. And then when the makeup was done, and we pulled a wig over their heads, they would look in the mirror and the expression on their faces was always identical. It was, "Gee, I am pretty."

—J. Roy Helland,
Hair and Makeup Design

The only setback at the beginning was when I told them they would all be wearing heels, and they thought I was talking about those little clunky shoes. But I said, "No, I want five-inch heels." And the first week was really tough for them because they'd never been in anything like that before. I said, "Look, the option is either you're going to look fabulous in these shoes, or you wear the little clunky shoes." So, they suffered through the pain, but that's the price of beauty, you know.

—Vincent Paterson, Choreographer

FOR SOME REASON, MEN IN DRESSES HAVE ALWAYS BEEN FUNNY. I don't know what it is, it just breaks everybody up.

—Mike Nichols

Drag queens have this incredible ability to be either outrageously funny or outrageously sexy. They're empowered because they totally transform themselves. I knew a little bit of that when I played Mrs. Doubtfire because you're freed, you can be someone else and inhabit her and play with it. I could change sexes without the painful operation.

—Robin Williams

Albert's a very highly strung performer, as many performers are, and enjoys being a star. The trick, I think, is how do you play this sort of outrageous character and maintain his humanity, and not make it all about the extremes?

—Nathan Lane

ABOUT THE CAST

ROBIN WILLIAMS (Armand Goldman) has excelled as both a great comedian and an outstanding dramatic actor, earning Academy Award nominations for his roles in *Good Morning, Vietnam; Dead Poets Society;* and *The Fisher King.* He has starred in such diverse films as *Mrs. Doubtfire, Awakenings* (National Board of Review award as Best Actor), *Moscow on the Hudson, Hook, The World According to Garp,* and *Jumanji,* and he won a special Golden Globe Award as the Genie in the animated hit musical *Aladdin.*

Born in Chicago, Williams grew up in northern California and then attended the Juilliard Academy in New York, where he spent three years under the tutelage of John Houseman, among others. Returning to the West Coast, he began performing at comedy clubs in San Francisco and Los Angeles. First gaining national attention on the television series *Happy Days* as the visiting alien Mork, he went on to star in the successful spin-off series *Mork and Mindy.*

Williams previously collaborated with director Mike Nichols on the revival of Samuel Beckett's *Waiting for Godot,* which enjoyed a sold-out run at New York's Lincoln Center.

GENE HACKMAN (Senator Keeley) has had an acting career that has spanned over three decades and encompassed more than fifty films.

In 1993 he won the Academy Award, the Golden Globe, the British Academy Award, and the Los Angeles and New York Film Critics awards for Best Supporting Actor for his work in Clint Eastwood's *Unforgiven.* Earlier in his career he won a Best Actor Oscar for his indelible portrayal of tough cop Popeye Doyle in *The French Connection* and earned a Best Actor Oscar nomination for his performance as a federal agent in *Mississippi Burning,* as well as two more Supporting Actor nominations for his work in *Bonnie and Clyde* and *I Never Sang for My Father.*

Some of Hackman's other recent films include *Get Shorty, Crimson Tide,* and *The Firm,* and his career list includes *The Poseidon Adventure, The Conversation, Young Frankenstein, A Bridge Too Far, Superman, Reds, Under Fire, Hoosiers, No Way Out,* and *Postcards from the Edge.*

Hackman recently returned to his New York stage roots when he starred in Mike Nichols's theatrical production of *Death and the Maiden,* also starring Glenn Close and Richard Dreyfuss.

NATHAN LANE (Albert) received the Drama Desk and Outer Critics Circle awards as well as a Tony Award for his performance in the hit revival of the musical *A Funny*

Thing Happened on the Way to the Forum. He has been acclaimed for his work in the Broadway plays *Love! Valour! Compassion!,* in which he reprised his role from the original Off-Broadway production; *Laughter on the 23rd Floor; Present Laughter; On Borrowed Time; Some Americans Abroad; Merlin; The Wind in the Willows;* and *Guys and Dolls.*

In 1992 Lane received an Obie Award for Sustained Excellence for his work in a variety of Off-Broadway productions. His extensive credits include the Terrence McNally plays *The Lisbon Traviata; Bad Habits;* and *Lips Together, Teeth Apart;* as well as *The Film Society; In a Pig's Valise; She Stoops to Conquer;* and *Measure for Measure,* directed by Joseph Papp for the New York Shakespeare Festival.

Among his screen and television credits Lane has voiced the role of Timon in the animated feature *The Lion King,* been nominated for an American Comedy Award for his appearance in *Jeffrey* and, most recently, starred in the Hallmark Hall of Fame presentation of *The Boys Next Door.*

DIANNE WIEST (Louise Keeley) won the Oscar for her portrayal of a flamboyant stage actress in Woody Allen's *Bullets Over Broadway.* She had previously won an Academy Award for her role in Allen's *Hannah and Her Sisters* and was also Oscar nominated for *Parenthood.*

Wiest made her feature film debut in Claudia Weill's *It's My Turn* and has gone on to appear in such movies as *I'm Dancing As Fast As I Can, Falling in Love, Edward Scissorhands, Little Man Tate, The Purple Rose of Cairo, September,* and *Radio Days.* She is presently starring in Peter Cohn's *Drunks,* which was screened at the 1996 Sundance Film Festival. The festival also honored the actress personally with the Piper Heidsieck Tribute for Independent Vision.

An accomplished stage actress, Wiest won the Obie, Clarence Derwent, and Theatre World awards for Best Actress for her performance in Tina Howe's *The Art of Dining.* She has also starred in *In the Summer House,* presented at Lincoln Center.

HANK AZARIA (Agador) has appeared on-screen in the movies *Heat, Quiz Show,* and *Pretty Woman.* His television credits include a starring role in the CBS romantic comedy *If Not for You,* with Elizabeth McGovern. He is also the voice of several key characters on Fox's long-running comedy series *The Simpsons* and starred in Fox's innovative sitcom *Herman's Head.*

Azaria trained at the American Academy of Dramatic Arts in New York and played the title role in a production of *Hamlet* at Columbia University. He continued his theater studies at Tufts University, where he appeared in productions of *Uncle Vanya, The Merchant of Venice, The Ballad of the Sad Cafe,* and *The Dumb Waiter.*

In Los Angeles, he worked in improvisation and sketch comedy and cowrote *An*

Evening on Thin Ice, which was presented at The Comedy Store. Azaria also won a DramaLogue Award for his work in the play *Conspicuous Consumption.*

CHRISTINE BARANSKI (Katharine) won an Emmy for her portrayal of Cybill Shepherd's wisecracking best friend in the CBS series *Cybill.* However, she has long delighted New York theater audiences in a wide variety of stage roles. Though *The Birdcage* marks her first screen collaboration with Mike Nichols, she had previously worked with the director in the Broadway production of Tom Stoppard's *The Real Thing,* for which she won a Tony Award and a Drama Desk Award. Nichols also directed her on Broadway in David Rabe's *Hurlyburly.* Baranski won a second Tony Award for her work in Neil Simon's *Rumors* and a Drama Desk Award for Terrence McNally's *Lips Together, Teeth Apart.* She starred in the Broadway presentation of John Guare's *House of Blue Leaves.*

On the screen Baranski has appeared in *Jeffrey, Reversal of Fortune, Addams Family Values, Life With Mikey, 9 ½ Weeks, Lovesick,* and *Legal Eagles.* She has also been seen in the television movies *Playing for Time* and *To Dance With the White Dog.*

DAN FUTTERMAN (Val Goldman) performed his first major role in a studio feature film in *The Birdcage.* He was previously seen in *The Fisher King, Big Girls Don't Cry,* and *Passed Away.*

A graduate of Columbia University, Futterman has earned praise for his work on the New York stage. He appeared in the award-winning Broadway play *Angels in America* and the Lincoln Center production of *The Lights.* He also had roles in such Off-Broadway plays as *The Raft of Medusa* and *Club Soda.*

On television, Futterman was featured in *The Out of Towners* and *Class of '61.*

CALISTA FLOCKHART (Barbara Keeley) won the Theater World and Clarence Derwent awards for her New York stage performance as Laura in *The Glass Menagerie* at the Roundabout Theater. She also earned praise for her work in the Off-Broadway production of *The Loop.*

Her other credits include Off-Broadway presentations of *All for One, Sophistry, Wrong Turn at Lungfish, Beside Herself,* and *Bower Boys.* In addition to her New York work, Flockhart has starred in several prominent regional productions, including *The Three Sisters* at Chicago's Goodman Theater and *Our Town* and *Death Takes a Holiday* at the Williamstown Theater Festival.

Flockhart has also been seen on-screen in the features *Quiz Show, Naked in New York,* and *Drunks,* and in the television movies *Darrow* and *The Secret Life of Mary Margaret Carter.*

ABOUT THE FILMMAKERS

MIKE NICHOLS (Director/Producer), during the course of his distinguished career, has won an Oscar, an Emmy, seven Tony Awards, and a Directors Guild Award, among many other honors.

Born in Berlin, Nichols emigrated with his family to New York in 1939 to escape Nazi persecution. He attended the University of Chicago, studied acting with Lee Strasberg in New York, and helped form the Compass Players, which evolved into the innovative Second City, where his colleagues included Elaine May, Alan Arkin, Shelley Berman, Barbara Harris, Zohra Lampert, and others. In 1957, Nichols and May launched their comedy partnership, which lasted for four years and included a yearlong, sold-out Broadway engagement.

Nichols began directing for the stage, making his Broadway debut in 1963 with the Neil Simon comedy *Barefoot in the Park*, which gained him his first Tony Award. He went on to direct a string of critical and commercial successes, including the Neil Simon hits *The Odd Couple, Plaza Suite*, and *Prisoner of Second Avenue*, all of which were honored with Tony Awards. He directed the Tony-winning *The Knack, Luv*, and *The Apple Tree*, as well as *Streamers*, voted Best Play by the New York Drama Critics, and the Pulitzer Prize-winning *The Gin Game*.

Other stage directorial credits include the Broadway productions of Tom Stoppard's Tony-winning *The Real Thing*, David Rabe's *Hurlyburly*, the comedy *Social Security*, Ariel Dorfman's *Death and the Maiden*, and the Lincoln Center revival of Samuel Beckett's *Waiting for Godot*. He also produced the hit Broadway musical *Annie*, which won seven Tony Awards, and Whoopi Goldberg's 1984 one-woman show, which first brought her national attention.

Already established as an award-winning Broadway stage director, Nichols made an auspicious feature film directorial debut with the screen version of Edward Albee's *Who's Afraid of Virginia Woolf?* and earned his first Best Director Academy Award nomination for his work on the film, which was also nominated for Best Picture and brought Oscars to actresses Elizabeth Taylor and Sandy Dennis. The following year Nichols won the Oscar for his direction of *The Graduate*, which was also nominated for Best Picture.

Nichols has since earned Academy Award nominations for Best Director for his work on *Silkwood* and *Working Girl*, which was also nominated for Best Picture. Among his other screen credits are *Catch 22, Carnal Knowledge, The Day of the Dolphin, The Fortune, Heartburn, Biloxi Blues, Postcards from the Edge, Regarding Henry*, and *Wolf*.

ELAINE MAY (Screenwriter) has enjoyed a multifaceted career as a highly regarded writer, director, and performer. She was honored with an Academy Award nomination for Best Screenplay for the comedy *Heaven Can Wait*, which she cowrote with the film's star Warren Beatty. She made her feature film directorial debut on *A New Leaf*, which she also scripted. She wrote and directed *Mikey and Nicky* and *Ishtar* and directed *The Heartbreak Kid* from a screenplay by Neil Simon, a film that earned a Best Supporting Actress Oscar nomination for her daughter, Jeannie Berlin.

Plays May has written for the stage include *Adaptation, Not Enough Rope, Mr. Gogol and Mr. Preen,* and the one-act play *Hot Line,* presented as part of the 1995 Off-Broadway hit *Death Defying Acts.* She also directed the Off-Broadway production of Terrence McNally's *Adaptation/Next.*

May has acted on-screen in such films as *Luv, Enter Laughing, A New Leaf, California Suite,* and *In the Spirit.* As a child she toured in several plays with her father, Yiddish stage actor Jack Berlin. At the University of Chicago, May met Mike Nichols, and both were founders of the trail-blazing Compass Players, which later became Second City. The duo went on to create one of the most successful comedy acts of the day. Together they headlined *An Evening With Nichols and May* on Broadway for a successful year long run, in addition to appearing at cabaret clubs around the country.

NEIL MACHLIS (Executive Producer) previously worked with Mike Nichols as the executive producer on *Postcards from the Edge* and *Wolf.* He also executive produced the hit comedies *Honeymoon in Vegas; Trains, Planes and Automobiles;* and *Chances Are.* In addition, Machlis served as the coproducer on such films as *I.Q., Three Men and a Little Lady, An Innocent Man,* and *Monster Squad.*

A graduate of the first class of the Directors Guild Training Program, Machlis worked his way up through the ranks from second assistant director to first assistant director and then to production manager and associate producer. His early credits as associate producer or production manager include such diverse films as *Grease, Grease 2, American Gigolo, Mommie Dearest, Johnny Dangerously, 2010,* and *Gung Ho.*

MARCELLO DANON (Executive Producer) has enjoyed a successful career extending over the last half of this century. He was the producer of the original French/Italian film *La Cage aux Folles.*

Danon began his career in the late 1940s working as an executive producer for several of the top film companies in France and Italy. In 1955 he produced his first film under his own production banner, Da.Ma. Films. Since then he has produced more than fifty films, including *Rififi, Chez les Hommes, En Cas de Malheur,* and the sequels to *OSS 117, Fantomas,* and *La Cage aux Folles.*

Danon has seen a number of his films honored with a variety of international awards, including the Golden Globe, César (France), David di Donatello (Italy), and nominations for the Academy Award and Special Jury Prize at the Cannes Film Festival.

EMMANUEL LUBEZKI (Director of Photography) most recently served as the cinematographer for *A Little Princess,* continuing a successful collaboration with director Alfonso Cuaron that began at the National University in Mexico City. One of Mexico's most esteemed directors of photography, Lubezki won his first Ariel Award in 1992 for his work on Alfonso Arau's *Like Water for Chocolate,* becoming the youngest recipient of that country's highest cinematography award. He won another Ariel for *Miroslava* the following year, and his third in 1994 for his work on *Amber,* making Lubezki the first person ever to be recognized with the Ariel for three consecutive years.

Lubezki again worked with Alfonso Arau on the recent hit romance *A Walk in the Clouds,* starring Keanu Reeves. His additional film credits include Alfonso Cuaron's feature film debut *Love in the Time of Hysteria,* as well as *Reality Bites, The Harvest,* and *Twenty Bucks.* He also won a Cable ACE Award for his work on the *Murder Obliquely* installment of the Showtime series *Fallen Angels.*

BO WELCH (Production Designer) previously worked with Mike Nichols on *Wolf* and worked with director Tim Burton on the films *Edward Scissorhands,* for which he won a BAFTA Award; *Beetlejuice;* and *Batman Returns.* He most recently served as the production designer as well as the second unit director on *A Little Princess,* which brought him the 1995 L.A. Film Critics Award for Best Art Director. His additional film credits include *Grand Canyon, The Accidental Tourist, Joe Versus the Volcano,* and *The Lost Boys.*

Prior to making the transition to production designer, Welch had been honored with an Academy Award nomination for his art direction on *The Color Purple.* Earlier in his career he worked as an art director on such films as *Swing Shift, Mommie Dearest, Chilly Scenes of Winter,* and *The Star Chamber.*

ARTHUR SCHMIDT (Editor) has won two Academy Awards, for director Robert Zemeckis's *Forrest Gump* and *Who Framed Roger Rabbit?.* In addition, Schmidt edited Zemeckis's three *Back to the Future* movies, as well as *Death Becomes Her.*

Among his other film credits are *Addams Family Values, Last of the Mohicans, Ruthless*

People, The Rocketeer, Fandango, The Escape Artist, Firstborn, Coal Miner's Daughter, and *Marathon Man.* Earlier in his career he worked with Mike Nichols as the assistant editor on *The Fortune.*

For television, Schmidt earned an Emmy Award as well as an Eddie Award for his work on the television film *The Jericho Mile.*

ANN ROTH (Costume Designer) continues a longtime association with Mike Nichols that began on Broadway and continued on-screen. She has created the costumes for the director's last seven films: *Wolf, Regarding Henry, Postcards from the Edge, Working Girl, Biloxi Blues, Heartburn,* and *Silkwood.* They also collaborated on the stage productions of *The Odd Couple, Lunch Hour, Social Security,* and the Lincoln Center revival of *Waiting for Godot.*

Her screen credits include more than forty films in a career that spans more than three decades. She received an Oscar nomination for her work on *Places in the Heart* and won the British Academy Award for *The Day of the Locust.* She has also designed the costumes for *Sabrina, Dave, Q & A, Pacific Heights, The Unbearable Lightness of Being, Jagged Edge, The World According to Garp, Dressed to Kill, Nine to Five, Hair, Coming Home, The Goodbye Girl,* and *Midnight Cowboy.*

For television, Roth's credits include *Serving in Silence* and *O Pioneer!* She also continues to divide her time between the stage and screen and recently designed the costumes for the New York productions of *Singin' in the Rain* and *Arms and the Man.*

VINCENT PATERSON (Choreographer) was recognized with a Tony Award nomination for his choreography of the musical adaptation of *Kiss of the Spiderwoman* on Broadway. For the concert stage he directed and choreographed Madonna's *Blonde Ambition* tour and Michael Jackson's *Bad* tour.

Paterson is currently choreographing the long-awaited film adaptation of the Broadway smash *Evita,* and his other film credits include *Hook* and *Havana.* He conceived, choreographed, and codirected the *Smooth Criminal* number in Michael Jackson's film *Moonwalker.* He has worked on music videos for Van Halen, Paul McCartney, George Harrison, and David Lee Roth, and his choreography has been seen in the award-winning commercials *Barkley of Seville* for Nike, Ray Charles's *Uh Huh* for Diet Pepsi, and the Levi's Loose campaign.

Paterson both directed and choreographed the TNT special *In Search of Dr. Seuss,* which earned seven Emmy nominations, including Best Choreography, and five ACE Award nominations, including Best Director.

UNITED ARTISTS PICTURES
Presents
A MIKE NICHOLS Film

ROBIN WILLIAMS   NATHAN LANE
GENE HACKMAN   DIANNE WIEST

THE BIRDCAGE

HANK AZARIA   WITH
CHRISTINE BARANSKI   CALISTA FLOCKHART
DAN FUTTERMAN   TOM McGOWAN

Casting by   Production Designer
JULIET TAYLOR and ELLEN LEWIS   BO WELCH

Associate Producer   Director of Photography
MICHELE IMPERATO   EMMANUEL LUBEZKI

Choreography by   Executive Producers
VINCENT PATERSON   NEIL MACHLIS
                                 and MARCELLO DANON
Costumes Designed by
ANN ROTH   Screenplay by
                                 ELAINE MAY
Edited by
ARTHUR SCHMIDT   Produced and Directed by
                                 MIKE NICHOLS

featuring   Live Music Arranged and Supervised by
GRANT HESLOV   Steven Goldstein
JAMES LALLY   Based on the stage play
Music Arranged and Adapted by   *La Cage aux Folles,* by Jean Poiret,
Jonathan Tunick   and the script written by Francis Veber,
                                 Edouard Molinaro, Marcello Danon, and Jean Poiret

Unit Production Managers .... Neil Machlis
                              Michele Imperato
First Assistant Director .... Joel Tuber
Second Assistant Director .... Jeff Okabayashi
Hair And Makeup Designs .... J. Roy Helland
                                 Peter Owen
Script Supervisor .... Mary Bailey
Supervising Sound Editor .... Ron Bochar
Re-Recording Mixer .... Lee Dichter
Associate Costume Designer .... Robert deMora
Art Director .... Tom Duffield
Set Decorator .... Cheryl Carasik
Assistant Art Director .... John Dexter
Camera Operator .... Rodrigo Garcia
First Assistant Camera .... Brian Armstrong
Second Assistant Camera .... Harry Zimmerman
Steadicam Operators .... P. Scott Sakimoto
                                 Rusty Geller
Video Assist Operator .... Brad Ralston

Associate Editor .... Kris Cole
First Assistant Editor .... Jeremiah O'Driscoll
Assistant Editor .... Dana Glauberman
Apprentice Editor .... Kurt Ramschissel
Production Sound Mixer ..... Gene Cantamessa C.A.S.
Boom Operators .... Raul Bruce
                                 Mark Jennings
The Birdcage Theatrical Lighting Designed by
John Tedesco and Jules Fisher
Chief Lighting Technician .... Dayton Nietert
Assistant Lighting Technician .... Thomas Nead
Rigging Gaffer .... Richard Smock
Key Grip .... Bob Gray
Second Company Grip .... Kenny King
Dolly Grip .... Alan Shultz
Rigging Grip .... Richard Crompton
Dialogue Editors .... Laura Civiello
                                 Magdaline Volaitis
                                 Philip Stockton

Sound Effects Editor	Lewis Goldstein
Foley Supervisor	Bruce Pross
Foley Editors	Steven Visscher
	Kam Chan
	Stuart Stanley
Foley Artist	Marko Costanza
Assistant Sound Editors	Nicholas Renbeck
	Dan Evans Farkas
Apprentice Sound Editor	Kimberly R. McCord
Sound Effects Recordist	Ben Cheah
ADR Supervisor	Deborah Wallach
ADR Assistant Editor	Kristen M. Johnson
Music Editor	Nick Meyers
Assistant Music Editors	Robert Nichols
	Nic Ratner
Supervising Music Engineer	Robert Schaper, Jr.
Scoring Mixer	Alan Silverman
Music Contractor	Seymour Red Press
Additional Orchestrations	Aaron Zigman
	Mort Lindsey
Post Production Supervisor	Paul A. Levin
Costume Supervisors	Cheryl Beasley Blackwell
	Bruce Ericksen
Mr. Williams's Costumer	Stephen Shubin
Wardrobe	David Mayreis
Wardrobe Assistant	Sabrina Calley
Key Makeup	Cheri Minns
Makeup	James McCoy
Ms. Baranski's Makeup	David Syner
Key Hairstylist	Carol O'Connell
Mr. Hackman's Stylist	Ron Scott
Ms. Baranski's Stylist	Baker
Hairstylist	Mary Ann Valdes
Assistant Choreographer	Smith Wordes
Location Manager	Robbie Goldstein
Second Second Assistant Director	Mark Tobey
Property Master	Mark Wade
Assistant Property Master	Randy Gunter
Art Department Coordinator	Stephanie Schwartzman
Leadman	David Manhan
Set Designer	Sean Haworth
Construction Coordinator	Michael Diersing
Construction Foreman	Brent Regan
Paint Supervisor	Clyde Zimmerman
Stand-by Painter	Nick Bridwell
Special Effects Coordinator	Stan Parks
Special Effects	Dan Sudick
Assistant to Mr. Nichols	Elizabeth Massie
Assistant to Mr. Machlis	Catherine Schwenn
Assistant to Mr. Williams	Rebecca Erwin Spencer
Production Coordinator	Carolyn Hagan
Assistant Production Coordinator	Patti McGuire

Production Accountant	Barbara Gutman
First Assistant Accountant	Kelly Richards Ralston
Production Secretary	Harry Winters
Unit Publicist	Doug Taylor
Production Assistants	Jonathan Capra
	Ian Hobbs
	Cricky Long
	John Pontrelli
Casting Assistants	Patricia Kerrigan
	Gail Goldberg
Extras Casting	John Laccetti
Extras Casting Assistant	Barbara Klein
Still Photographer	Lorey Sebastian
Loader	Stephanie Maislen
Catering	Michael Schultz
Craft Service	Monique Limery
Transportation Coordinator	Dan Marrow
Transportation Captain	Randy Burke

Miami Crew

Location Manager	Adolfo Calderon
2nd Assistant Director	Marten W. Piccinini
Production Coordinator	Elayne Schneiderman
Props	Charles Guanci, Jr.
Transportation Captain	Larry Crenshaw
Extras Casting	Ellen Jacoby
Catering	TomKats, Inc.
Special Visual Effects by	Syd Dutton and Bill Taylor, A.S.C. of Illusion Arts, Inc.

Visual Effects Crew

Digital Supervisor	Richard Patterson
Optical/Digital Photography	David S. Williams, Jr.
Matte Artists	Robert Stromberg
	Mike Wassel
Digital Adviser	Mark Sawicki
Matte Photography	Adam Kowalski
Special Rigging	Lynn Ledgerwood
Production Manager	Catherine Sudolcan
Hammerhead Animator	Rebecca Marie
CISSGI Artists/Operators	Gregory Oehler
	Ron Kallsen
	Larry Gaynor

CAST

Armand Goldman	Robin Williams
Senator Keeley	Gene Hackman
Albert	Nathan Lane
Louise Keeley	Dianne Wiest
Val Goldman	Dan Futterman
Barbara Keeley	Calista Flockhart
Agador	Hank Azaria
Katharine	Christine Baranski
Harry Radman	Tom McGowan
Photographer	Grant Heslov
Chauffeur	Kirby Mitchell
Cyril	James Lally

Celsius .... Luca Tommassini
The Goldman Girls .... Luis Camacho
André Fuentes
Anthony Richard Gonzalez
Dante Lamar Henderson
Scott Kaske
Kevin Alexander Stea
Waiter in Club ....Tim Kelleher
TV Woman in Van .... Ann Cusack
TV Man in Van .... Stanley DeSantis
Club Hostess.. J. Roy Helland
Fishmonger ....Anthony Giaimo
Bakery Man .... Lee Delano
Senator Eli Jackson ....David Sage
TV Hosts .... Mike Kinsley
Tony Snow
Keeleys' Maid...............................Dorothy Constantine
Black Girl on TV .... Trina McGee-Davis
TV Reporters .... Barry Nolan
Amy Powell
Ron Pitts
James Hill
Mary Major
State Trooper.. Steven Porfido
Waiter in Cafe .... John D. Pontrelli
Big Guy in Park ....Herschel Sparber
Katharine's Secretary ....Francesca Cruz
TV Editors ....Brian Reddy
Jim Jansen
Latino Man in Club .... Al Rodrigo
Matrons ....Marjorie Lovett
Sylvia Short
Pastor..James H. Morrison
Rabbi .... Rabbi Robert K. Baruch
Mr. Williams's Stand-in........................... Adam Bryant
Mr. Hackman's Stand-in................ Gregory B. Goossen
Stunt Coordinator .... Jery Hewitt
Utility Stunts .... George Palmiero
Scott Howell
Helicopter Pilot .... Cliff Fleming

THE PRODUCERS WISH TO THANK:
The City Of Miami Beach, Florida
Zomba Music

"La Virgen Lloraba"
Written by Lupe Yoli
Performed by La Lupe
Courtesy of Sonido Records

"Conga"
Written By Enrique E. Garcia
Performed by Gloria Estefan and Miami Sound Machine
Courtesy of Epic Records
By arrangement with Sony Music

"Mi Guajira"
Written by Israel "Cachao" Lopez
Performed by Cachao
Courtesy of Crescent Moon Records, Inc.
By arrangement with Sony Music

"Lady Marmalade"
Written by Bob Crewe and Kenny Nolan

"She Works Hard for the Money"
Written by Donna Summer and Michael Omartian
Courtesy of Mercury Records
By arrangement with PolyGram Film & TV licensing

"Say It Again"
Written by Steven Goldstein, Val Garay, and
Anthony Lapoe
Performed by Planet One
Courtesy of Aarol Music

"The Man That Got Away"
Written by Ira Gershwin and Harold Arlen
Courtesy of Capitol Records
By arrangement with CEMA Special Markets

"I Could Have Danced All Night"
Written by Alan Lerner and Frederick Loewe

"We Are Family"
Written by Bernard Edwards and Nile Rodgers

"Little Dream"
Written by Stephen Sondheim

"Love Is in the Air"
Written by Stephen Sondheim

"Can That Boy Fox Trot"
Written by Stephen Sondheim

"To the Foundation"
Written by Carlton Hines

Titles and Opticals by............................ Pacific Title
Negative Cutter.. Mo Henry
Color Timer .... Bob Kaiser
DTS Consultant .... Jeff Levison

Camera Cranes and Dollies by Chapman
Spacecam Aerial Camera System provided by
Spacecam Systems, Inc.

Filmed at Paramount Studios, Hollywood, California
Greenwich Studios, North Miami, Florida
and in part at Ren-Mar Studios, Hollywood, California

Sound Post Production at C5, Inc., N.Y.
Re-Recorded at Sound One Corp., N.Y.
Color and Release Prints by Technicolor®